THE LIFE OF
KING HENRY the FIFTH
BY WILLIAM SHAKESPEARE

Edited by

GEORGE LYMAN KITTREDGE

GINN AND COMPANY
BOSTON · NEW YORK · CHICAGO

LONDON · ATLANTA · DALLAS · COLUMBUS · SAN FRANCISCO

𝔗𝔥𝔢 𝔄𝔱𝔥𝔢𝔫𝔞𝔲𝔪 𝔓𝔯𝔢𝔰𝔰

GINN AND COMPANY · PRO-
PRIETORS · BOSTON · U.S.A.

PREFACE

THE TEXT is complete and agrees with that in Kittredge's edition of Shakespeare's *Works*. The numbering of the lines accords with that commonly used in citing the plays. This method is preferred to a new counting in order to facilitate reference to such standard works as Bartlett's *Concordance* and Schmidt's *Shakespeare-Lexicon*. In prose passages there results some slight irregularity in computation, but this does not indicate any omission in the text.

The explanatory notes were found, practically complete, among the papers of the late Professor Kittredge. They have been edited by a former student of Kittredge's, Professor Arthur Colby Sprague of Bryn Mawr College, who is wholly responsible for the textual notes and the glossary.

CONTENTS

INTRODUCTION

HENRY THE FIFTH is mentioned in the Stationers' Register on August 4, 1600, and the formal entry, by Thomas Pavyer, comes ten days later. The First Quarto (1600) offers a garbled text of a drastically cut-down version. The Second Quarto (1602) was printed from the First; and so, apparently, was the Third, which, though dated 1608, was in fact published in 1619. The First Folio contains the play in its full and authentic form. Bad as it is, the First Quarto enables one to correct a good many of the Folio's misprints. Three lines not found in the Folio appear to be genuine and are supplied from the Quarto in the present text (ii, 1, 110–111; iv, 3, 48). The most famous of all Shakespearean emendations is Theobald's correction of the Folio reading 'and a Table of greene fields' (ii, 3, 17), which makes no sense, to 'and 'a babbled of green fields.' The Quartos omit the words.

The proper division into acts is shown by the Chorus in each case. In the Quarto (which omits the speeches of the Chorus) there is no division. The Folio marks the acts, but in some instances erroneously.

The date of HENRY THE FIFTH is fixed with unusual exactness by the reference to Essex in the Chorus to Act V:

> Were now the general of our gracious Empress
> (As in good time he may) from Ireland coming,
> Bringing rebellion broached on his sword,
> How many would the peaceful city quit
> To welcome him!

Essex left London on March 27, 1599, reached Dublin in April, and, returning from a campaign which was a complete fiasco, arrived at London on September 28 in the same year. Meres, in his *Palladis Tamia*, published in the autumn of 1598, mentions *Henry the Fourth*, but not HENRY THE FIFTH. The play is promised in the Epilogue to *Henry the Fourth, Part II.*

For history Shakespeare relies for the most part on Holinshed's *Chronicle. The Famous Victories of Henry the Fifth* includes most of the reign, ending with the betrothal to Katherine of France, which took place on May 21, 1420. From this old play Shakespeare took hints for the action and he sometimes echoes its phrases. Thus, in the famous anecdote of the tennis balls (i, 2, 234 ff.), the king's eloquent reply to the Dauphin's insulting message is quite original; but there are traces of both Holinshed and the old play. In the play we have: 'My lord prince Dolphin is very pleasant with me: but tel him, that in steed of balles of leather, we wil tose him balles of brasse and yron, yea such balles as never were tost in France, the proudest tennis court shall rue it. . . . Therefore get thee hence, and tel him thy message quickly, lest I be there before thee: away priest, be gone.' In Holinshed: 'The K[ing] wrote to him, [the Dauphin,] that yer ought long, he would tosse him some London balles that perchance should shake the walles of the best court in France.'

The French nobles are not well treated by Shakespeare. Their rather vulgar frivolity is distasteful to the modern reader, who looks at the situation impartially, and not with the eyes of a patriotic Elizabethan. Holinshed tells us simply that the French, confident of victory, 'made great triumph; for the capteins had determined before how to diuide the spoile, and the soldiers the night before had plaid the Englishmen at dice.' The old play dramatizes Holinshed. It brings in three soldiers and a drummer playing at dice and speaking broken English; also a captain who has 'set three or foure chaire makers a worke, to make a new disguised chaire to set that womanly King of England in, that all the people may laugh and scoffe at him.' Yet he pities the 'poore English scabs': 'Why, take an English man out of his warme bed and his stale drinke, but one moneth, and alas what wil become of him? But giue the Frenchman a Reddish roote, and he wil liue with it all the dayes of his life.' (Cf. iii, 7, 93, 158 ff.; iv, Chorus, 17–22.) Alençon is of much the same opinion in *1 Henry VI*, i, 2, 9–12:

> They want their porridge and their fat bull-beeves.
> Either they must be dieted like mules
> And have their provender tied to their mouths,
> Or piteous they will look, like drowned mice.

The way in which Shakespeare picked up phrases is well illustrated in the Prologue:

> Then should the warlike Harry, like himself,
> Assume the port of Mars, and at his heels
> (Leash'd in, like hounds) should famine, sword, and fire
> Crouch for employment.

In Holinshed King Henry uses a similar figure in reply to an ambassador from the besieged citizens of Rouen: 'He declared that the goddesse of battell, called *Bellona*, had three handmaidens, euer of necessitie attending vpon her, as blood, fire, and famine.' Cf. also the exhortation of the Archbishop of Canterbury (i, 2, 131): 'With blood and sword and fire to win your right.' Canterbury's long address in explanation of King Henry's title to the crown of France (i, 2, 35–100) is simply versified from Holinshed, with only such slight changes as are needed to transfer prose into blank verse. Indeed, Shakespeare found in Holinshed's prose four or five lines which he could take over as verse without the change of a word. This illustrates the fallacy of any argument based on the discovery of so-called 'verse fossils' in prose passages.

The Quarto omits the Prologue and all other speeches of the Chorus. Some of these furnish historical information that the audience cannot do without. Incidentally, they are interesting documents in the history of dramatic criticism. They express, over and over again, the doctrine of the voluntary subjection of our minds to the illusion of the stage (as opposed to dramatic deception)—a principle which a succession of eminent critics arrived at by a long course of study and debate, and which Schlegel and Coleridge are often thought to have finally worked out.

The character of Henry V in this play is inconsistent with the character of the Prince in *Henry the Fourth*. The difference is not moral, but mental. The Prince has a brilliant intellect that works with flashing rapidity; King Henry's mind is not inferior, but it is of another order: it is strong and sure, but does not scintillate. No such mental transformation could result from a reform in manners and morals. The inconsistency is, of course, in no sense a fault in Shakespeare's portrayal. He was quite at liberty to give different accounts of the same personage in different plays. For the intensely religious nature of King Henry, Shakespeare had ample justification in Holinshed, and he has emphasized it throughout, so that the conquest of France becomes to all intents and purposes a holy war.

THE LIFE OF
KING HENRY
THE FIFTH

[Dramatis Personæ

Chorus.

King Henry the Fifth.
Duke of Gloucester, } brothers to the *King.*
Duke of Bedford,
Duke of Exeter, uncle to the *King.*
Duke of York, cousin to the *King.*
Earl of Salisbury.
Earl of Westmoreland.
Earl of Warwick.
Archbishop of Canterbury.
Bishop of Ely.
Earl of Cambridge.
Lord Scroop.
Sir Thomas Grey.
Sir Thomas Erpingham,
Gower, an English captain,
Fluellen, a Welsh captain, } officers in *King Henry's* army.
Macmorris, an Irish captain,
Jamy, a Scottish captain,
John Bates,
Alexander Court, } soldiers in the same.
Michael Williams,
Pistol.
Nym.
Bardolph.
Boy.
A Herald.

Charles the Sixth, King of France.
Lewis, the Dauphin.
Duke of Burgundy.
Duke of Orleans.
Duke of Bourbon.
The Constable of France.
Rambures,
Grandpré, } French lords.
Beaumont,
Governor of Harfleur.
Montjoy, a French herald.
Ambassadors to the *King of England.*

Isabel, Queen of France.
Katherine, daughter to *Charles* and *Isabel.*
Alice, a lady attending on her.
Hostess of the Boar's Head tavern in Eastcheap (formerly *Mistress Quickly,* now married to *Pistol*).

Lords, Ladies, Officers, Soldiers, Citizens, Messengers, and Attendants.

SCENE.—*England and France.*]

THE LIFE OF
KING HENRY
THE FIFTH

Enter *Prologue.*

O for a Muse of fire, that would ascend
The brightest heaven of invention,
A kingdom for a stage, princes to act,
And monarchs to behold the swelling scene!
Then should the warlike Harry, like himself,   5
Assume the port of Mars, and at his heels
(Leash'd in, like hounds) should famine, sword, and fire
Crouch for employment. But pardon, gentles all,
The flat unraised spirits that have dar'd
On this unworthy scaffold to bring forth   10
So great an object. Can this cockpit hold
The vasty fields of France? Or may we cram
Within this wooden O the very casques
That did affright the air at Agincourt?
O, pardon! since a crooked figure may   15
Attest in little place a million,
And let us, ciphers to this great accompt,
On your imaginary forces work.
Suppose within the girdle of these walls
Are now confin'd two mighty monarchies,   20
Whose high-upreared and abutting fronts
The perilous narrow ocean parts asunder.
Piece out our imperfections with your thoughts:
Into a thousand parts divide one man
And make imaginary puissance.   25
Think, when we talk of horses, that you see them
Printing their proud hoofs i' th' receiving earth.
For 'tis your thoughts that now must deck our kings,

Carry them here and there, jumping o'er times,
Turning th' accomplishment of many years   30
Into an hourglass; for the which supply,
Admit me Chorus to this history,
Who, Prologue-like, your humble patience pray,
Gently to hear, kindly to judge our play.   *Exit.*

ACT I. Scene I. [*London. An antechamber in the* King's *Palace.*]

Enter the two *Bishops*—[*the Archbishop*] *of Canterbury*
and [*the Bishop of*] *Ely.*

Cant. My lord, I'll tell you, that self bill is urg'd
Which in th' eleventh year of the last king's reign
Was like, and had indeed against us pass'd
But that the scambling and unquiet time
Did push it out of farther question.   5
  Ely. But how, my lord, shall we resist it now?
  Cant. It must be thought on. If it pass against us,
We lose the better half of our possession;
For all the temporal lands which men devout
By testament have given to the Church   10
Would they strip from us; being valu'd thus—
As much as would maintain, to the King's honour,
Full fifteen earls and fifteen hundred knights,
Six thousand and two hundred good esquires,
And, to relief of lazars and weak age,   15
Of indigent faint souls, past corporal toil,
A hundred almshouses right well supplied;
And to the coffers of the King beside,
A thousand pounds by th' year. Thus runs the bill.
  Ely. This would drink deep.
  Cant.   'Twould drink the cup and all. 20

Ely. But what prevention?

Cant. The King is full of grace and fair regard.

Ely. And a true lover of the holy Church.

Cant. The courses of his youth promis'd it not.
The breath no sooner left his father's body   25
But that his wildness, mortified in him,
Seem'd to die too. Yea, at that very moment
Consideration like an angel came
And whipp'd th' offending Adam out of him,
Leaving his body as a paradise   30
T' envelop and contain celestial spirits.
Never was such a sudden scholar made;
Never came reformation in a flood
With such a heady currance scouring faults;
Nor never hydra-headed wilfulness   35
So soon did lose his seat, and all at once,
As in this king.

Ely.   We are blessed in the change.

Cant. Hear him but reason in divinity,
And, all-admiring, with an inward wish
You would desire the King were made a prelate;   40
Hear him debate of commonwealth affairs,
You would say it hath been all in all his study;
List his discourse of war, and you shall hear
A fearful battle rend'red you in music;
Turn him to any cause of policy,   45
The Gordian knot of it he will unloose,
Familiar as his garter; that, when he speaks,
The air, a charter'd libertine, is still,
And the mute wonder lurketh in men's ears
To steal his sweet and honey'd sentences;   50
So that the art and practic part of life
Must be the mistress to this theoric;

Which is a wonder how his Grace should glean it,
Since his addiction was to courses vain,
His companies unletter'd, rude, and shallow,   55
His hours fill'd up with riots, banquets, sports;
And never noted in him any study,
Any retirement, any sequestration
From open haunts and popularity.

Ely. The strawberry grows underneath the nettle,   60
And wholesome berries thrive and ripen best
Neighbour'd by fruit of baser quality;
And so the Prince obscur'd his contemplation
Under the veil of wildness, which (no doubt)
Grew like the summer grass, fastest by night,   65
Unseen, yet crescive in his faculty.

Cant. It must be so; for miracles are ceas'd,
And therefore we must needs admit the means
How things are perfected.

Ely.   But, my good lord,
How now for mitigation of this bill   70
Urg'd by the commons? Doth his Majesty
Incline to it, or no?

Cant.   He seems indifferent;
Or rather swaying more upon our part
Than cherishing th' exhibiters against us;
For I have made an offer to his Majesty—   75
Upon our spiritual Convocation,
And in regard of causes now in hand,
Which I have open'd to his Grace at large,
As touching France—to give a greater sum
Than ever at one time the clergy yet   80
Did to his predecessors part withal.

Ely. How did this offer seem receiv'd, my lord?

Cant. With good acceptance of his Majesty;

Save that there was not time enough to hear,
As I perceiv'd his Grace would fain have done,   85
The severals and unhidden passages
Of his true titles to some certain dukedoms,
And generally to the crown and seat of France,
Deriv'd from Edward, his great-grandfather.
     Ely. What was th' impediment that broke this off?   90
     Cant. The French ambassador upon that instant
Crav'd audience; and the hour I think is come
To give him hearing. Is it four o'clock?
     Ely. It is.
     Cant. Then go we in to know his embassy,   95
Which I could with a ready guess declare
Before the Frenchman speak a word of it.
     Ely. I'll wait upon you, and I long to hear it.   *Exeunt.*

[Scene II. *London. The presence chamber in the Palace.*]

     Enter the *King, Humphrey* [*Duke of Gloucester*], *Bedford,
Clarence, Warwick, Westmoreland,* and *Exeter,* [with *Attendants*].

     King. Where is my gracious Lord of Canterbury?
     Exe. Not here in presence.
     King.   Send for him, good uncle.
     West. Shall we call in th' ambassador, my liege?
     King. Not yet, my cousin. We would be resolv'd,
Before we hear him, of some things of weight,   5
That task our thoughts, concerning us and France.

     Enter two *Bishops*—[the *Archbishop of Canterbury*
                and the *Bishop of Ely*].

     Cant. God and his angels guard your sacred throne
And make you long become it!

King.   Sure we thank you.
My learned lord, we pray you to proceed
And justly and religiously unfold   10
Why the Law Salique, that they have in France,
Or should or should not bar us in our claim.
And God forbid, my dear and faithful lord,
That you should fashion, wrest, or bow your reading,
Or nicely charge your understanding soul   15
With opening titles miscreate whose right
Suits not in native colours with the truth;
For God doth know how many, now in health,
Shall drop their blood in approbation
Of what your reverence shall incite us to.   20
Therefore take heed how you impawn our person,
How you awake our sleeping sword of war.
We charge you in the name of God, take heed;
For never two such kingdoms did contend
Without much fall of blood, whose guiltless drops   25
Are every one a woe, a sore complaint
'Gainst him whose wrong gives edge unto the swords
That make such waste in brief mortality.
Under this conjuration speak, my lord;
For we will hear, note, and believe in heart   30
That what you speak is in your conscience wash'd
As pure as sin with baptism.
    Cant. Then hear me, gracious sovereign, and you peers,
That owe yourselves, your lives, and services
To this imperial throne. There is no bar   35
To make against your Highness' claim to France
But this which they produce from Pharamond:
'In terram Salicam mulieres ne succedant';
'No woman shall succeed in Salique land.'
Which Salique land the French unjustly gloze   40

To be the realm of France, and Pharamond
The founder of this law and female bar.
Yet their own authors faithfully affirm
That the land Salique is in Germany,
Between the floods of Sala and of Elbe;   45
Where Charles the Great, having subdu'd the **Saxons,**
There left behind and settled certain French;
Who, holding in disdain the German women
For some dishonest manners of their life,
Establish'd then this law: to wit, no female   50
Should be inheritrix in Salique land;
Which Salique (as I said) 'twixt Elbe and Sala
Is at this day in Germany call'd Meisen.
Then doth it well appear the Salique Law
Was not devised for the realm of France;   55
Nor did the French possess the Salique land
Until four hundred one and twenty years
After defunction of King Pharamond,
Idly suppos'd the founder of this law,
Who died within the year of our redemption   60
Four hundred twenty-six; and Charles the Great
Subdu'd the Saxons, and did seat the French
Beyond the river Sala, in the year
Eight hundred five. Besides, their writers say,
King Pepin, which deposed Childeric,   65
Did, as heir general, being descended
Of Blithild, which was daughter to King Clothair,
Make claim and title to the crown of France.
Hugh Capet also—who usurp'd the crown
Of Charles the Duke of Lorraine, sole heir male   70
Of the true line and stock of Charles the Great—
To fine his title with some shows of truth,
Though in pure truth it was corrupt and naught,

Convey'd himself as heir to th' Lady Lingare,
Daughter to Charlemain, who was the son   75
To Lewis the Emperor, and Lewis the son
Of Charles the Great. Also King Lewis the Tenth,
Who was sole heir to the usurper Capet,
Could not keep quiet in his conscience,
Wearing the crown of France, till satisfied   80
That fair Queen Isabel, his grandmother,
Was lineal of the Lady Ermengare,
Daughter to Charles the foresaid Duke of Lorraine;
By the which marriage the line of Charles the Great
Was reunited to the crown of France.   85
So that, as clear as is the summer's sun,
King Pepin's title and Hugh Capet's claim,
King Lewis his satisfaction, all appear
To hold in right and title of the female.
So do the kings of France unto this day,   90
Howbeit they would hold up this Salique Law
To bar your Highness claiming from the female,
And rather choose to hide them in a net
Than amply to imbare their crooked titles
Usurp'd from you and your progenitors.   95
    King. May I with right and conscience make this claim?
    Cant. The sin upon my head, dread sovereign!
For in the Book of Numbers is it writ:
When the man dies, let the inheritance
Descend unto the daughter. Gracious lord,   100
Stand for your own, unwind your bloody flag,
Look back into your mighty ancestors;
Go, my dread lord, to your great-grandsire's tomb,
From whom you claim; invoke his warlike spirit,
And your great-uncle's, Edward the Black Prince,   105

Who on the French ground play'd a tragedy,
Making defeat on the full power of France,
Whiles his most mighty father on a hill
Stood smiling to behold his lion's whelp
Forage in blood of French nobility.   110
O noble English, that could entertain
With half their forces the full pride of France
And let another half stand laughing by,
All out of work and cold for action!

    Ely. Awake remembrance of these valiant dead   115
And with your puissant arm renew their feats.
You are their heir; you sit upon their throne;
The blood and courage that renowned them
Runs in your veins; and my thrice-puissant liege
Is in the very May-morn of his youth   120
Ripe for exploits and mighty enterprises.

    Exe. Your brother kings and monarchs of the earth
Do all expect that you should rouse yourself,
As did the former lions of your blood.

    West. They know your Grace hath cause and means and
        might;   125
So hath your Highness. Never king of England
Had nobles richer and more loyal subjects,
Whose hearts have left their bodies here in England
And lie pavilion'd in the fields of France.

    Cant. O, let their bodies follow, my dear liege,   130
With blood and sword and fire, to win your right!
In aid whereof we of the spiritualty
Will raise your Highness such a mighty sum
As never did the clergy at one time
Bring in to any of your ancestors.   135

    King. We must not only arm t' invade the French,

But lay down our proportions to defend
Against the Scot, who will make road upon us
With all advantages.

    Cant. They of those marches, gracious sovereign,   140
Shall be a wall sufficient to defend
Our inland from the pilfering borderers.

    King. We do not mean the coursing snatchers only,
But fear the main intendment of the Scot,
Who hath been still a giddy neighbour to us;   145
For you shall read that my great-grandfather
Never went with his forces into France
But that the Scot on his unfurnish'd kingdom
Came pouring like the tide into a breach,
With ample and brim fulness of his force,   150
Galling the gleaned land with hot assays,
Girding with grievous siege castles and towns;
That England, being empty of defence,
Hath shook and trembled at th' ill neighbourhood.

    Cant. She hath been then more fear'd than harm'd, my liege;
For hear her but exampled by herself: 156
When all her chivalry hath been in France,
And she a mourning widow of her nobles,
She hath herself not only well defended
But taken and impounded as a stray   160
The King of Scots; whom she did send to France
To fill King Edward's fame with prisoner kings,
And make her chronicle as rich with praise
As is the ooze and bottom of the sea
With sunken wrack and sumless treasuries.   165

    West. But there's a saying very old and true—
            'If that you will France win,
            Then with Scotland first begin.'
For once the eagle (England) being in prey,

To her unguarded nest the weasel (Scot)   170
Comes sneaking, and so sucks her princely eggs,
Playing the mouse in absence of the cat,
To spoil and havoc more than she can eat.
    Exe. It follows then, the cat must stay at home.
Yet that is but a curst necessity,   175
Since we have locks to safeguard necessaries,
And pretty traps to catch the petty thieves.
While that the armed hand doth fight abroad,
Th' advised head defends itself at home;
For government, though high, and low, and lower,   180
Put into parts, doth keep in one consent,
Congreeing in a full and natural close,
Like music.
    Cant.   True! Therefore doth heaven divide
The state of man in divers functions,
Setting endeavour in continual motion;   185
To which is fixed as an aim or butt
Obedience; for so work the honeybees,
Creatures that by a rule in nature teach
The act of order to a peopled kingdom.
They have a king, and officers of sorts,   190
Where some like magistrates correct at home,
Others like merchants venture trade abroad,
Others like soldiers armed in their stings
Make boot upon the summer's velvet buds,
Which pillage they with merry march bring home   195
To the tent-royal of their emperor,
Who, busied in his majesty, surveys
The singing masons building roofs of gold,
The civil citizens kneading up the honey,
The poor mechanic porters crowding in   200
Their heavy burthens at his narrow gate,

The sad-ey'd justice, with his surly hum,
Delivering o'er to executors pale
The lazy yawning drone. I this infer,
That many things having full reference   205
To one consent may work contrariously,
As many arrows loosed several ways
Come to one mark, as many ways meet in one town,
As many fresh streams meet in one salt sea,
As many lines close in the dial's centre;   210
So may a thousand actions, once afoot,
End in one purpose, and be all well borne
Without defeat. Therefore to France, my liege!
Divide your happy England into four,
Whereof take you one quarter into France,   215
And you withal shall make all Gallia shake.
If we, with thrice such powers left at home,
Cannot defend our own doors from the dog,
Let us be worried, and our nation lose
The name of hardiness and policy.   220
    King. Call in the messengers sent from the Dauphin.
                              [*Exeunt some Attendants.*]
Now are we well resolv'd, and by God's help
And yours, the noble sinews of our power,
France being ours, we'll bend it to our awe,
Or break it all to pieces. Or there we'll sit,   225
Ruling in large and ample empery
O'er France and all her (almost) kingly dukedoms,
Or lay these bones in an unworthy urn,
Tombless, with no remembrance over them.
Either our history shall with full mouth   230
Speak freely of our acts, or else our grave,
Like Turkish mute, shall have a tongueless mouth,
Not worshipp'd with a waxen epitaph.

Enter Ambassadors *of France, [attended].*

Now are we well prepar'd to know the pleasure
Of our fair cousin Dauphin; for we hear   235
Your greeting is from him, not from the King.
   Ambassador. May't please your Majesty to give us leave
Freely to render what we have in charge;
Or shall we sparingly show you far off
The Dauphin's meaning, and our embassy?   240
   King. We are no tyrant, but a Christian king,
Unto whose grace our passion is as subject
As are our wretches fett'red in our prisons.
Therefore with frank and with uncurbed plainness
Tell us the Dauphin's mind.
   Ambassador.   Thus then, in few: 245
Your Highness, lately sending into France,
Did claim some certain dukedoms, in the right
Of your great predecessor, King Edward the Third.
In answer of which claim, the Prince our master
Says that you savour too much of your youth,   250
And bids you be advis'd. There's naught in France
That can be with a nimble galliard won;
You cannot revel into dukedoms there.
He therefore sends you, meeter for your spirit,
This tun of treasure; and, in lieu of this,   255
Desires you let the dukedoms that you claim
Hear no more of you. This the Dauphin speaks.
   King. What treasure, uncle?
   Exe.   Tennis balls, my liege.
   King. We are glad the Dauphin is so pleasant with us.
His present and your pains we thank you for.   260
When we have match'd our rackets to these balls,
We will in France (by God's grace) play a set
Shall strike his father's crown into the hazard.

Tell him he hath made a match with such a wrangler
That all the courts of France will be disturb'd   265
With chases. And we understand him well,
How he comes o'er us with our wilder days,
Not measuring what use we made of them.
We never valu'd this poor seat of England,
And therefore, living hence, did give ourself   270
To barbarous license; as 'tis ever common
That men are merriest when they are from home.
But tell the Dauphin I will keep my state,
Be like a king, and show my sail of greatness,
When I do rouse me in my throne of France.   275
For that I have laid by my majesty
And plodded like a man for working days.
But I will rise there with so full a glory
That I will dazzle all the eyes of France,
Yea, strike the Dauphin blind to look on us.   280
And tell the pleasant Prince this mock of his
Hath turn'd his balls to gunstones, and his soul
Shall stand sore charged for the wasteful vengeance
That shall fly with them; for many a thousand widows
Shall this his mock mock out of their dear husbands,   285
Mock mothers from their sons, mock castles down;
And some are yet ungotten and unborn
That shall have cause to curse the Dauphin's scorn.
But this lies all within the will of God,
To whom I do appeal, and in whose name,   290
Tell you the Dauphin, I am coming on,
To venge me as I may and to put forth
My rightful hand in a well-hallow'd cause.
So get you hence in peace. And tell the Dauphin
His jest will savour but of shallow wit   295
When thousands weep more than did laugh at it.

Convey them with safe conduct. Fare you well.

Exeunt Ambassadors.

   Exe. This was a merry message.

   King. We hope to make the sender blush at it.

Therefore, my lords, omit no happy hour   300

That may give furth'rance to our expedition;

For we have now no thought in us but France,

Save those to God, that run before our business.

Therefore let our proportions for these wars

Be soon collected, and all things thought upon   305

That may with reasonable swiftness add

More feathers to our wings; for, God before,

We'll chide this Dauphin at his father's door.

Therefore let every man now task his thought

That this fair action may on foot be brought.   310

Exeunt.

Flourish. Enter *Chorus.*

Now all the youth of England are on fire,
And silken dalliance in the wardrobe lies.
Now thrive the armourers, and honour's thought
Reigns solely in the breast of every man.
They sell the pasture now to buy the horse,   5
Following the mirror of all Christian kings
With winged heels, as English Mercuries.
For now sits Expectation in the air
And hides a sword, from hilts unto the point,
With crowns imperial, crowns, and coronets   10
Promis'd to Harry and his followers.
The French, advis'd by good intelligence
Of this most dreadful preparation,
Shake in their fear and with pale policy
Seek to divert the English purposes.   15
O England! model to thy inward greatness,
Like little body with a mighty heart,
What mightst thou do that honour would thee do,
Were all thy children kind and natural!
But see thy fault! France hath in thee found out   20
A nest of hollow bosoms, which he fills
With treacherous crowns; and three corrupted men—
One, Richard Earl of Cambridge, and the second,
Henry Lord Scroop of Masham, and the third,
Sir Thomas Grey, knight, of Northumberland—   25
Have, for the gilt of France (O guilt indeed!)
Confirm'd conspiracy with fearful France,
And by their hands this grace of kings must die,
If hell and treason hold their promises,
Ere he take ship for France, and in Southampton.   30

Linger your patience on, and well digest
Th' abuse of distance. Force a play!
The sum is paid, the traitors are agreed,
The King is set from London, and the scene
Is now transported, gentles, to Southampton.   35
There is the playhouse now, there must you sit,
And thence to France shall we convey you safe
And bring you back, charming the narrow seas
To give you gentle pass; for, if we may,
We'll not offend one stomach with our play.   40
But, till the King come forth, and not till then,
Unto Southampton do we shift our scene.   *Exit.*

[Scene I. *London. A street.*]

Enter *Corporal Nym* and *Lieutenant Bardolph.*

Bard. Well met, Corporal Nym.

Nym. Good morrow, Lieutenant Bardolph.

Bard. What, are Ancient Pistol and you friends yet?   4

Nym. For my part, I care not. I say little; but when time shall serve, there shall be smiles—but that shall be as it may. I dare not fight; but I will wink and hold out mine iron. It is a simple one; but what though? It will toast cheese, and it will endure cold as another man's sword will—and there's an end.   11

Bard. I will bestow a breakfast to make you friends, and we'll be all three sworn brothers to France. Let't be so, good Corporal Nym.

Nym. Faith, I will live so long as I may, that's the certain of it; and when I cannot live any longer, I will do as I may. That is my rest, that is the rendezvous of it.

Bard. It is certain, Corporal, that he is married to Nell Quickly, and certainly she did you wrong, for you were troth-plight to her.   21

Nym. I cannot tell. Things must be as they may. Men may sleep, and they may have their throats about them at that time, and some say knives have edges. It must be as it may. Though patience be a tired mare, yet she will plod. There must be con-clusions. Well, I cannot tell. 27

Enter *Pistol* and *Hostess Quickly*.

Bard. Here comes Ancient Pistol and his wife. Good Cor-poral, be patient here. How now, mine host Pistol? 30

Pist. Base tyke, call'st thou me host?
Now by this hand I swear I scorn the term;
Nor shall my Nell keep lodgers!

Host. No, by my troth, not long; for we cannot lodge and board a dozen or fourteen gentlewomen that live honestly by the prick of their needles but it will be thought we keep a bawdy house straight. [*Nym and Pistol draw.*] O well-a-day, Lady, if he be not drawn now! We shall see wilful adultery and murther committed. 40

Bard. Good Lieutenant—good Corporal—offer nothing here.

Nym. Pish!

Pist. Pish for thee, Iceland dog! thou prick-ear'd cur of Iceland!

Host. Good Corporal Nym, show thy valour, and put up your sword. 46

Nym. Will you shog off? I would have you solus.

Pist. 'Solus,' egregrious dog? O viper vile!
The 'solus' in thy most mervailous face!
The 'solus' in thy teeth, and in thy throat,
And in thy hateful lungs, yea, in thy maw, perdy!
And, which is worse, within thy nasty mouth!
I do retort the 'solus' in thy bowels;
For I can take, and Pistol's cock is up, 55
And flashing fire will follow.

Nym. I am not Barbason; you cannot conjure me. I have an humour to knock you indifferently well. If you grow foul with me, Pistol, I will scour you with my rapier, as I may, in fair terms. If you would walk off, I would prick your guts a little in good terms, as I may, and that's the humour of it.

Pist. O braggard vile, and damned furious wight,
The grave doth gape, and doting death is near.
Therefore exhale!   66

Bard. Hear me, hear me what I say! He that strikes the first stroke, I'll run him up to the hilts, as I am a soldier. . [*Draws.*]

Pist. An oath of mickle might, and fury shall abate.   70
                              [*Pistol and Nym sheathe their swords.*]
Give me thy fist, thy forefoot to me give.
Thy spirits are most tall.

Nym. I will cut thy throat one time or other in fair terms.
That is the humour of it.

Pist. Couple a gorge!   75
That is the word. I thee defy again.
O hound of Crete, think'st thou my spouse to get?
No; to the spital go,
And from the powd'ring tub of infamy
Fetch forth the lazar kite of Cressid's kind,   80
Doll Tearsheet, she by name, and her espouse.
I have, and I will hold, the quondam Quickly
For the only she; and—pauca, there's enough.
Go to!   84

Enter the *Boy.*

Boy. Mine host Pistol, you must come to my master—and you, hostess. He is very sick and would to bed. Good Bardolph, put thy face between his sheets and do the office of a warming pan. Faith, he's very ill.

Bard. Away, you rogue!   90

Host. By my troth, he'll yield the crow a pudding one of these days. The King has kill'd his heart. Good husband, come home presently.   *Exit [with Boy].*

Bard. Come, shall I make you two friends? We must to France together. Why the devil should we keep knives to cut one another's throats?   96

Pist. Let floods o'erswell, and fiends for food howl on!

Nym. You'll pay me the eight shillings I won of you at betting?

Pist. Base is the slave that pays.   100

Nym. That now I will have. That's the humour of it.

Pist. As manhood shall compound. Push home.

They draw.

Bard. By this sword, he that makes the first thrust, I'll kill him! By this sword, I will.   [*Draws.*]   105

Pist. 'Sword' is an oath, and oaths must have their course.

[*Sheathes his sword.*]

Bard. Corporal Nym, an thou wilt be friends, be friends; an thou wilt not, why then be enemies with me too. Prithee put up.

Nym. I shall have my eight shillings I won of you at betting?

Pist. A noble shalt thou have, and present pay;
And liquor likewise will I give to thee,
And friendship shall combine, and brotherhood.
I'll live by Nym, and Nym shall live by me.   115
Is not this just? For I shall sutler be
Unto the camp, and profits will accrue.
Give me thy hand.

[*Nym sheathes his sword.*]

Nym. I shall have my noble?

Pist. In cash, most justly paid.   120

Nym. Well then, that's the humour of 't.

[*They shake hands.*]

Enter *Hostess*.

Host. As ever you came of women, come in quickly to Sir
John. Ah, poor heart! he is so shak'd of a burning quotidian
tertian that it is most lamentable to behold. Sweet men, come
to him.   126

Nym. The King hath run bad humours on the knight; that's
the even of it.

Pist. Nym, thou hast spoke the right.
His heart is fracted and corroborate.   130

Nym. The King is a good king, but it must be as it may.
He passes some humours and careers.

Pist. Let us condole the knight; for, lambkins, we will live.
                                                        Exeunt.

[Scene II. *Southampton. A council chamber.*]

Enter *Exeter*, *Bedford*, and *Westmoreland*.

Bed. Fore God, his Grace is bold to trust these traitors.

Exe. They shall be apprehended by-and-by.

West. How smooth and even they do bear themselves,
As if allegiance in their bosoms sat,
Crowned with faith and constant loyalty!   5

Bed. The King hath note of all that they intend,
By interception which they dream not of.

Exe. Nay, but the man that was his bedfellow,
Whom he hath dull'd and cloy'd with gracious favours—
That he should, for a foreign purse, so sell   10
His sovereign's life to death and treachery!

Sound trumpets. Enter the *King*, *Scroop*, *Cambridge*, and *Grey*,
          [*Lords*, and *Attendants*].

King. Now sits the wind fair, and we will aboard.
My Lord of Cambridge, and my kind Lord of Masham,

And you, my gentle knight, give me your thoughts.
Think you not that the pow'rs we bear with us   15
Will cut their passage through the force of France,
Doing the execution and the act
For which we have in head assembled them?
   Scroop. No doubt, my liege, if each man do his best.
   King. I doubt not that, since we are well persuaded   20
We carry not a heart with us from hence
That grows not in a fair consent with ours,
Nor leave not one behind that doth not wish
Success and conquest to attend on us.
   Cam. Never was monarch better fear'd and lov'd   25
Than is your Majesty. There's not, I think, a subject
That sits in heart-grief and uneasiness
Under the sweet shade of your government.
   Grey. True. Those that were your father's enemies
Have steep'd their galls in honey and do serve you   30
With hearts create of duty and of zeal.
   King. We therefore have great cause of thankfulness,
And shall forget the office of our hand
Sooner than quittance of desert and merit
According to the weight and worthiness.   35
   Scroop. So service shall with steeled sinews toil,
And labour shall refresh itself with hope,
To do your Grace incessant services.
   King. We judge no less. Uncle of Exeter,
Enlarge the man committed yesterday   40
That rail'd against our person. We consider
It was excess of wine that set him on,
And on his more advice, we pardon him.
   Scroop. That's mercy, but too much security
Let him be punish'd, sovereign, lest example   45
Breed (by his sufferance) more of such a kind.

King. O, let us yet be merciful!
Cam. So may your Highness, and yet punish too.
Grey. Sir,
You show great mercy if you give him life   50
After the taste of much correction.
    King. Alas, your too much love and care of me
Are heavy orisons 'gainst this poor wretch!
If little faults proceeding on distemper
Shall not be wink'd at, how shall we stretch our eye   55
When capital crimes, chew'd, swallow'd, and digested,
Appear before us? We'll yet enlarge that man,
Though Cambridge, Scroop, and Grey, in their dear care
And tender preservation of our person,
Would have him punish'd. And now to our French causes. 60
Who are the late commissioners?
    Cam. I one, my lord.
Your Highness bade me ask for it to-day.
    Scroop. So did you me, my liege.
    Grey. And I, my royal sovereign.   65
    King. Then, Richard Earl of Cambridge, there is yours;
There yours, Lord Scroop of Masham; and, Sir Knight,
Grey of Northumberland, this same is yours.
Read them, and know I know your worthiness.
My Lord of Westmoreland, and uncle Exeter,   70
We will aboard to-night.—Why how now, gentlemen?
What see you in those papers that you lose
So much complexion?—Look ye, how they change!
Their cheeks are paper.—Why, what read you there
That hath so cowarded and chas'd your blood   75
Out of appearance?
    Cam.   I do confess my fault,
And do submit me to your Highness' mercy.
    Grey, Scroop. To which we all appeal.

King. The mercy that was quick in us but late,
By your own counsel is suppress'd and kill'd.   80
You must not dare (for shame) to talk of mercy;
For your own reasons turn into your bosoms
As dogs upon their masters, worrying you.
See you, my princes and my noble peers,
These English monsters! My Lord of Cambridge here—   85
You know how apt our love was to accord
To furnish him with all appertinents
Belonging to his honour; and this man
Hath, for a few light crowns, lightly conspir'd
And sworn unto the practices of France   90
To kill us here in Hampton; to the which
This knight, no less for bounty bound to us
Than Cambridge is, hath likewise sworn. But O,
What shall I say to thee, Lord Scroop, thou cruel,
Ingrateful, savage, and inhuman creature?   95
Thou that didst bear the key of all my counsels,
That knew'st the very bottom of my soul,
That (almost) mightst have coin'd me into gold,
Wouldst thou have practis'd on me for thy use—
May it be possible that foreign hire   100
Could out of thee extract one spark of evil
That might annoy my finger? 'Tis so strange
That, though the truth of it stands off as gross
As black and white, my eye will scarcely see it.
Treason and murther ever kept together,   105
As two yoke-devils sworn to either's purpose,
Working so grossly in a natural cause
That admiration did not whoop at them;
But thou ('gainst all proportion) didst bring in
Wonder to wait on treason and on murther;   110
And whatsoever cunning fiend it was

That wrought upon thee so preposterously
Hath got the voice in hell for excellence.
All other devils that suggest by treasons
Do botch and bungle up damnation 115
With patches, colours, and with forms being fetch'd
From glist'ring semblances of piety;
But he that temper'd thee bade thee stand up,
Gave thee no instance why thou shouldst do treason,
Unless to dub thee with the name of traitor. 120
If that same demon that hath gull'd thee thus
Should with his lion gait walk the whole world,
He might return to vasty Tartar back
And tell the legions, 'I can never win
A soul so easy as that Englishman's.' 125
O, how hast thou with jealousy infected
The sweetness of affiance! Show men dutiful?
Why, so didst thou. Seem they grave and learned?
Why, so didst thou. Come they of noble family?
Why, so didst thou. Seem they religious? 130
Why, so didst thou. Or are they spare in diet,
Free from gross passion or of mirth or anger,
Constant in spirit, not swerving with the blood,
Garnish'd and deck'd in modest complement,
Not working with the eye without the ear, 135
And but in purged judgment trusting neither?
Such and so finely bolted didst thou seem;
And thus thy fall hath left a kind of blot
To mark the full-fraught man and best indu'd
With some suspicion. I will weep for thee; 140
For this revolt of thine, methinks, is like
Another fall of man. Their faults are open.
Arrest them to the answer of the law;
And God acquit them of their practices!

Exe. I arrest thee of high treason by the name of Richard Earl
of Cambridge.   146

I arrest thee of high treason by the name of Henry Lord
Scroop of Masham.

I arrest thee of high treason by the name of Thomas Grey,
knight, of Northumberland.   150

Scroop. Our purposes God justly hath discover'd,
And I repent my fault more than my death,
Which I beseech your Highness to forgive,
Although my body pay the price of it.

Cam. For me, the gold of France did not seduce,   155
Although I did admit it as a motive
The sooner to effect what I intended.
But God be thanked for prevention,
Which I in sufferance heartily will rejoice,
Beseeching God, and you, to pardon me.   160

Grey. Never did faithful subject more rejoice
At the discovery of most dangerous treason
Than I do at this hour joy o'er myself,
Prevented from a damned enterprise.
My fault, but not my body, pardon, sovereign.   165

King. God quit you in his mercy! Hear your sentence.
You have conspir'd against our royal person,
Join'd with an enemy proclaim'd, and from his coffers
Receiv'd the golden earnest of our death;
Wherein you would have sold your king to slaughter,   170
His princes and his peers to servitude,
His subjects to oppression and contempt,
And his whole kingdom into desolation.
Touching our person, seek we no revenge,
But we our kingdom's safety must so tender,   175
Whose ruin you have sought, that to her laws
We do deliver you. Get you therefore hence

(Poor miserable wretches) to your death;
The taste whereof God of his mercy give
You patience to endure, and true repentance   180
Of all your dear offences! Bear them hence.

              Exeunt [Cambridge, Scroop, and Grey, guarded].
Now, lords, for France; the enterprise whereof
Shall be to you as us, like glorious.
We doubt not of a fair and lucky war,
Since God so graciously hath brought to light   185
This dangerous treason, lurking in our way
To hinder our beginnings. We doubt not now
But every rub is smoothed on our way.
Then, forth, dear countrymen. Let us deliver
Our puissance into the hand of God,   190
Putting it straight in expedition.
Cheerly to sea; the signs of war advance.
No king of England, if not King of France!

                        Flourish. Exeunt.

[Scene III. *London. Before the Boar's Head Tavern, Eastcheap.*]

      Enter *Pistol, Nym, Bardolph, Boy,* and *Hostess.*

  Host. Prithee, honey-sweet husband, let me bring thee to
Staines.

  Pist. No; for my manly heart doth ern.
Bardolph, be blithe; Nym, rouse thy vaunting veins;
Boy, bristle thy courage up; for Falstaff he is dead,   5
And we must ern therefore.

  Bard. Would I were with him, wheresome'er he is, either in
heaven or in hell!

  Host. Nay sure, he's not in hell! He's in Arthur's bosom, if
ever man went to Arthur's bosom. 'A made a finer end, and
went away an it had been any christom child. 'A parted ev'n

just between twelve and one, ev'n at the turning o' th' tide.
For after I saw him fumble with the sheets, and play with
flowers, and smile upon his fingers' ends, I knew there was but
one way; for his nose was as sharp as a pen, and 'a babbled of
green fields. 'How now, Sir John?' quoth I. 'What, man? be
o' good cheer.' So 'a cried out 'God, God, God!' three or four
times. Now I, to comfort him, bid him 'a should not think of
God; I hop'd there was no need to trouble himself with any
such thoughts yet. So 'a bade me lay more clothes on his feet.
I put my hand into the bed and felt them, and they were as
cold as any stone. Then I felt to his knees, and so upward and
upward, and all was as cold as any stone.

Nym. They say he cried out of sack.

Host. Ay, that 'a did.   30

Bard. And of women.

Host. Nay, that 'a did not.

Boy. Yes, that 'a did, and said they were devils incarnate. 34

Host. 'A could never abide carnation; 'twas a colour he never
lik'd.

Boy. 'A said once the devil would have him about women.

Host. 'A did in some sort, indeed, handle women; but then
he was rheumatic, and talk'd of the Whore of Babylon.   41

Boy. Do you not remember 'a saw a flea stick upon Bardolph's
nose, and 'a said it was a black soul burning in hellfire?   44

Bard. Well, the fuel is gone that maintain'd that fire. That's
all the riches I got in his service.

Nym. Shall we shog? The King will be gone from Southampton.

Pist. Come, let's away. My love, give me thy lips.
Look to my chattels and my moveables.   50
Let senses rule. The word is 'Pitch and pay.'
Trust none;
For oaths are straws, men's faiths are wafer-cakes,

And Hold-fast is the only dog, my duck.
Therefore Caveto be thy counsellor.   55
Go, clear thy crystals. Yoke-fellows in arms,
Let us to France, like horse-leeches, my boys,
To suck, to suck, the very blood to suck!
   Boy. And that's but unwholesome food, they say.   60
   Pist. Touch her soft mouth, and march.
   Bard. Farewell, hostess.   [*Kisses her.*]
   Nym. I cannot kiss, that is the humour of it; but adieu!
   Pist. Let housewifery appear. Keep close, I thee command.
   Host. Farewell! adieu!   *Exeunt.*

[Scene IV. *France. The* French King's *Palace.*]

Flourish. Enter the *French King*, the *Dauphin*, the *Dukes of*
   Berri and *Britain*, [the *Constable*, and others].

   King. Thus comes the English with full power upon us,
And more than carefully it us concerns
To answer royally in our defences.
Therefore the Dukes of Berri and Britain,
Of Brabant and of Orleans, shall make forth,   5
And you, Prince Dauphin, with all swift dispatch,
To line and new repair our towns of war
With men of courage and with means defendant;
For England his approaches makes as fierce
As waters to the sucking of a gulf.   10
It fits us then to be as provident
As fear may teach us out of late examples
Left by the fatal and neglected English
Upon our fields.
   Dau.   My most redoubted father,
It is most meet we arm us 'gainst the foe;   15

For peace itself should not so dull a kingdom
(Though war nor no known quarrel were in question)
But that defences, musters, preparations
Should be maintain'd, assembled, and collected,
As were a war in expectation.   20
Therefore I say 'tis meet we all go forth
To view the sick and feeble parts of France;
And let us do it with no show of fear—
No, with no more than if we heard that England
Were busied with a Whitsun morris dance;   25
For, my good liege, she is so idly king'd,
Her sceptre so fantastically borne,
By a vain, giddy, shallow, humorous youth,
That fear attends her not.
    Con.   O peace, Prince Dauphin!
You are too much mistaken in this king.   30
Question your Grace the late ambassadors,
With what great state he heard their embassy,
How well supplied with noble counsellors,
How modest in exception, and withal
How terrible in constant resolution,   35
And you shall find his vanities forespent
Were but the outside of the Roman Brutus,
Covering discretion with a coat of folly;
As gardeners do with ordure hide those roots
That shall first spring and be most delicate.   40
    Dau. Well, 'tis not so, my Lord High Constable!
But though we think it so, it is no matter.
In cases of defence 'tis best to weigh
The enemy more mighty than he seems.
So the proportions of defence are fill'd;   45
Which of a weak and niggardly projection
Doth, like a miser, spoil his coat with scanting

A little cloth.
   King.   Think we King Harry strong;
And, princes, look you strongly arm to meet him.
The kindred of him hath been flesh'd upon us;   50
And he is bred out of that bloody strain
That haunted us in our familiar paths.
Witness our too much memorable shame
When Cressy battle fatally was struck,
And all our princes captiv'd, by the hand   55
Of that black name, Edward, Black Prince of Wales;
Whiles that his mountain sire—on mountain standing,
Up in the air, crown'd with the golden sun—
Saw his heroical seed, and smil'd to see him,
Mangle the work of nature, and deface   60
The patterns that by God and by French fathers
Had twenty years been made. This is a stem
Of that victorious stock; and let us fear
The native mightiness and fate of him.

Enter a Messenger.

   Mess. Ambassadors from Harry King of England   65
Do crave admittance to your Majesty.
   King. We'll give them present audience. Go, and bring
them.
                         [*Exeunt Messenger and certain Lords.*]
You see this chase is hotly followed, friends.
   Dau. Turn head, and stop pursuit; for coward dogs
Most spend their mouths when what they seem to threaten 70
Runs far before them. Good my sovereign,
Take up the English short, and let them know
Of what a monarchy you are the head.
Self-love, my liege, is not so vile a sin
As self-neglecting.

Enter [*Lords*, with] *Exeter* [and *Train*].

King.   From our brother England?   75
  Exe. From him, and thus he greets your Majesty:
He wills you, in the name of God Almighty,
That you devest yourself, and lay apart
The borrowed glories that by gift of heaven,
By law of nature and of nations, 'longs   80
To him and to his heirs—namely, the crown
And all wide-stretched honours that pertain
By custom, and the ordinance of times,
Unto the crown of France. That you may know
'Tis no sinister nor no awkward claim,   85
Pick'd from the wormholes of long-vanish'd days,
Nor from the dust of old oblivion rak'd,
He sends you this most memorable line,   [*Gives a paper.*]
In every branch truly demonstrative;
Willing you overlook this pedigree;   90
And when you find him evenly deriv'd
From his most fam'd of famous ancestors,
Edward the Third, he bids you then resign
Your crown and kingdom, indirectly held
From him, the native and true challenger.   95
  King. Or else what follows?
  Exe. Bloody constraint; for if you hide the crown
Even in your hearts, there will he rake for it.
Therefore in fiery tempest is he coming,
In thunder and in earthquake, like a Jove;   100
That, if requiring fail, he will compel;
And bids you, in the bowels of the Lord,
Deliver up the crown, and to take mercy
On the poor souls for whom this hungry war
Opens his vasty jaws; and on your head   105

Turns he the widows' tears, the orphans' cries,
The dead men's blood, the pining maidens' groans,
For husbands, fathers, and betrothed lovers
That shall be swallowed in this controversy.
This is his claim, his threat'ning, and my message;   110
Unless the Dauphin be in presence here,
To whom expressly I bring greeting too.
   King. For us, we will consider of this further.
To-morrow shall you bear our full intent
Back to our brother England.
   Dau.   For the Dauphin,   115
I stand here for him. What to him from England?
   Exe. Scorn and defiance, slight regard, contempt,
And anything that may not misbecome
The mighty sender, doth he prize you at.
Thus says my king: An if your father's Highness   120
Do not, in grant of all demands at large,
Sweeten the bitter mock you sent his Majesty,
He'll call you to so hot an answer of it
That caves and womby vaultages of France
Shall chide your trespass, and return your mock   125
In second accent of his ordinance.
   Dau. Say, if my father render fair return,
It is against my will; for I desire
Nothing but odds with England. To that end,
As matching to his youth and vanity,   130
I did present him with the Paris balls.
   Exe. He'll make your Paris Louvre shake for it,
Were it the mistress court of mighty Europe;
And be assur'd you'll find a difference,
As we his subjects have in wonder found,   135
Between the promise of his greener days
And these he masters now. Now he weighs time

Even to the utmost grain. That you shall read
In your own losses, if he stay in France.

    King. To-morrow shall you know our mind at full.   140

    Exe. Dispatch us with all speed, lest that our king
Come here himself to question our delay;
For he is footed in this land already.

    King. You shall be soon dispatch'd with fair conditions.
A night is but small breath and little pause   145
To answer matters of this consequence.

                                  Flourish.   *Exeunt.*

Enter *Chorus*.

Thus with imagin'd wing our swift scene flies,
In motion of no less celerity
Than that of thought. Suppose that you have seen
The well-appointed King at Hampton pier
Embark his royalty; and his brave fleet   5
With silken streamers the young Phœbus fanning.
Play with your fancies; and in them behold
Upon the hempen tackle shipboys climbing;
Hear the shrill whistle, which doth order give
To sounds confus'd; behold the threaden sails,   10
Borne with th' invisible and creeping wind,
Draw the huge bottoms through the furrowed sea,
Breasting the lofty surge. O, do but think
You stand upon the rivage and behold
A city on th' inconstant billows dancing;   15
For so appears this fleet majestical,
Holding due course to Harflew. Follow, follow!
Grapple your minds to sternage of this navy,
And leave your England as dead midnight still,
Guarded with grandsires, babies, and old women,   20
Either past or not arriv'd to pith and puissance;
For who is he whose chin is but enrich'd
With one appearing hair that will not follow
These cull'd and choice-drawn cavaliers to France?
Work, work your thoughts, and therein see a siege.   25
Behold the ordinance on their carriages,
With fatal mouths gaping on girded Harflew.
Suppose th' ambassador from the French comes back;
Tells Harry that the King doth offer him
Katherine his daughter, and with her to dowry   30

Some petty and unprofitable dukedoms.
The offer likes not; and the nimble gunner
With linstock now the devilish cannon touches,

Alarum, and chambers go off.

And down goes all before them. Still be kind,
And eke out our performance with your mind.   *Exit.*

[Scene I. *France. Before Harfleur.*]

Alarum. Enter the *King*, *Exeter*, *Bedford*, and *Gloucester*, [with
        Soldiers carrying] scaling ladders at Harflew.

  King. Once more unto the breach, dear friends, once more;
Or close the wall up with our English dead!
In peace there's nothing so becomes a man
As modest stillness and humility;
But when the blast of war blows in our ears,   5
Then imitate the action of the tiger:
Stiffen the sinews, summon up the blood,
Disguise fair nature with hard-favour'd rage;
Then lend the eye a terrible aspect;
Let it pry through the portage of the head   10
Like the brass cannon; let the brow o'erwhelm it
As fearfully as doth a galled rock
O'erhang and jutty his confounded base,
Swill'd with the wild and wasteful ocean.
Now set the teeth and stretch the nostril wide,   15
Hold hard the breath and bend up every spirit
To his full height! On, on, you noble English,
Whose blood is fet from fathers of war-proof!
Fathers that like so many Alexanders
Have in these parts from morn till even fought,   20
And sheath'd their swords for lack of argument.
Dishonour not your mothers; now attest

That those whom you call'd fathers did beget you!
Be copy now to men of grosser blood
And teach them how to war! And you, good yeomen,   25
Whose limbs were made in England, show us here
The mettle of your pasture. Let us swear
That you are worth your breeding; which I doubt not,
For there is none of you so mean and base
That hath not noble lustre in your eyes.   30
I see you stand like greyhounds in the slips,
Straining upon the start. The game's afoot!
Follow your spirit; and upon this charge
Cry 'God for Harry! England and Saint George!'
                    [*Exeunt.*] *Alarum, and chambers go off.*

[Scene II. *Before Harfleur.*]

Enter *Nym, Bardolph, Pistol,* and *Boy.*

Bard. On, on, on, on, on! to the breach, to the breach!

Nym. Pray thee, Corporal, stay. The knocks are too hot;
and, for mine own part, I have not a case of lives. The humour
of it is too hot; that is the very plain-song of it.   6

Pist. The plain-song is most just; for humours do abound.

    Knocks go and come; God's vassals drop and die;
        And sword and shield
          In bloody field   10
        Doth win immortal fame.

Boy. Would I were in an alehouse in London! I would give
all my fame for a pot of ale and safety.

Pist. And I: 15
        If wishes would prevail with me,
        My purpose should not fail with me,
        But thither would I hie.

Boy.   As duly, but not as truly,
        As bird doth sing on bough.   20

Enter *Fluellen*.

Flu. Up to the breach, you dogs! Avaunt, you cullions!

[*Drives them forward.*]

Pist. Be merciful, great duke, to men of mould!
Abate thy rage, abate thy manly rage,
Abate thy rage, great duke!   25
Good bawcock, bate thy rage! Use lenity, sweet chuck!

Nym. These be good humours. Your honour wins bad humours.

Exeunt [*all but Boy*].

Boy. As young as I am, I have observ'd these three swashers.
I am boy to them all three; but all they three, though they
would serve me, could not be man to me; for indeed three such
antics do not amount to a man. For Bardolph, he is white-
liver'd and red-fac'd; by the means whereof 'a faces it out, but
fights not. For Pistol, he hath a killing tongue and a quiet
sword; by the means whereof 'a breaks words and keeps whole
weapons. For Nym, he hath heard that men of few words are
the best men, and therefore he scorns to say his prayers, lest 'a
should be thought a coward; but his few bad words are match'd
with as few good deeds, for 'a never broke any man's head but
his own, and that was against a post when he was drunk. They
will steal anything, and call it purchase. Bardolph stole a lute-
case, bore it twelve leagues, and sold it for three halfpence.
Nym and Bardolph are sworn brothers in filching, and in Calais
they stole a fire-shovel. I knew by that piece of service the men
would carry coals. They would have me as familiar with men's
pockets as their gloves or their handkerchers; which makes
much against my manhood, if I should take from another's
pocket to put into mine; for it is plain pocketing up of wrongs.
I must leave them and seek some better service. Their villany
goes against my weak stomach, and therefore I must cast it up.

Exit.

Enter *Gower* [and *Fluellen*].

Gow. Captain Fluellen, you must come presently to the mines. The Duke of Gloucester would speak with you.   60

Flu. To the mines? Tell you the Duke, it is not so good to come to the mines; for look you, the mines is not according to the disciplines of the war. The concavities of it is not sufficient; for look you, th' athversary, you may discuss unto the Duke, look you, is digt himself four yard under the countermines. By Cheshu, I think 'a will plow up all, if there is not better directions.   68

Gow. The Duke of Gloucester, to whom the order of the siege is given, is altogether directed by an Irishman, a very valiant gentleman, i' faith.   71

Flu. It is Captain Macmorris, is it not?

Gow. I think it be.

Flu. By Cheshu, he is an ass, as in the world! I will verify as much in his beard. He has no more directions in the true disciplines of the wars, look you, of the Roman disciplines, than is a puppy-dog.

Enter *Macmorris* and *Captain Jamy*.

Gow. Here 'a comes, and the Scots captain, Captain Jamy, with him.   80

Flu. Captain Jamy is a marvellous falorous gentleman, that is certain, and of great expedition and knowledge in th' aunchiant wars, upon my particular knowledge of his directions. By Cheshu, he will maintain his argument as well as any military man in the world in the disciplines of the pristine wars of the Romans.

Jamy. I say gud day, Captain Fluellen.

Flu. God-den to your worship, good Captain James.   90

Gow. How now, Captain Macmorris? Have you quit the mines? Have the pioners given o'er?

Mac. By Chrish, la, tish ill done! The work ish give over, the trompet sound the retreat. By my hand I swear, and my father's soul, the work ish ill done! It ish give over. I would have blowed up the town, so Chrish save me la! in an hour. O, tish ill done! tish ill done! By my hand, tish ill done!   99

Flu. Captain Macmorris, I beseech you now, will you voutsafe me, look you, a few disputations with you, as partly touching or concerning the disciplines of the war, the Roman wars? In the way of argument, look you, and friendly communication; partly to satisfy my opinion, and partly for the satisfaction, look you, of my mind—as touching the direction of the military discipline, that is the point.   108

Jamy. It sall be vary gud, gud feith, gud Captens bath, and I sall quit you with gud leve, as I may pick occasion. That sall I, mary.

Mac. It is no time to discourse, so Chrish save me! The day is hot, and the weather, and the wars, and the King, and the Dukes. It is no time to discourse. The town is beseech'd, and the trompet call us to the breach, and we talk, and, be Chrish, do nothing. 'Tis shame for us all. So God sa' me, 'tis shame to stand still, it is shame, by my hand! and there is throats to be cut, and works to be done, and there ish nothing done, so Chrish sa' me, la!

Jamy. By the mess, ere theise eyes of mine take themselves to slomber, ay'll de gud service, or ay'll lig i' th' grund for it! ay, or go to death! And ay'll pay't as valorously as I may, that sall I surley do, that is the breff and the long. Mary, I wad full fain heard some question 'tween you tway.

Flu. Captain Macmorris, I think, look you, under your correction, there is not many of your nation—   131

Mac. Of my nation? What ish my nation? Ish a villain, and a basterd, and a knave, and a rascal. What ish my nation? Who talks of my nation?   135

Flu. Look you, if you take the matter otherwise than is meant, Captain Macmorris, peradventure I shall think you do not use me with that affability as in discretion you ought to use me, look you, being as good a man as yourself, both in the disciplines of war, and in the derivation of my birth, and in other particularities.

Mac. I do not know you so good a man as myself. So Chrish save me, I will cut off your head!   145

Gow. Gentlemen both, you will mistake each other.

Jamy. Ah, that's a foul fault!

A parley [sounded].

Gow. The town sounds a parley.   149

Flu. Captain Macmorris, when there is more better oportunity to be required, look you, I will be so bold as to tell you I know the disciplines of war; and there is an end.   *Exeunt.*

[Scene III. *Before the gates of Harfleur*.]

[Enter the *Governor* and some *Citizens* on the walls.]   Enter
     King [*Henry*] and all his *Train* before the gates.

King. How yet resolves the Governor of the town?
This is the latest parle we will admit.
Therefore to our best mercy give yourselves,
Or, like to men proud of destruction,
Defy us to our worst; for, as I am a soldier,   5
A name that in my thoughts becomes me best,
If I begin the batt'ry once again,
I will not leave the half-achieved Harflew
Till in her ashes she lie buried.
The gates of mercy shall be all shut up,   10
And the flesh'd soldier, rough and hard of heart,
In liberty of bloody hand shall range

With conscience wide as hell, mowing like grass
Your fresh fair virgins and your flow'ring infants.
What is it then to me if impious war,   15
Array'd in flames like to the prince of fiends,
Do with his smirch'd complexion all fell feats
Enlink'd to waste and desolation?
What is't to me, when you yourselves are cause,
If your pure maidens fall into the hand   20
Of hot and forcing violation?
What rein can hold licentious wickedness
When down the hill he holds his fierce career?
We may as bootless spend our vain command
Upon th' enraged soldiers in their spoil   25
As send precepts to the Leviathan
To come ashore. Therefore, you men of Harflew,
Take pity of your town and of your people
Whiles yet my soldiers are in my command,
Whiles yet the cool and temperate wind of grace   30
O'erblows the filthy and contagious clouds
Of heady murther, spoil, and villany.
If not—why, in a moment look to see
The blind and bloody soldier with foul hand
Defile the locks of your shrill-shrieking daughters;   35
Your fathers taken by the silver beards,
And their most reverend heads dash'd to the walls;
Your naked infants spitted upon pikes,
Whiles the mad mothers with their howls confus'd
Do break the clouds, as did the wives of Jewry   40
At Herod's bloody-hunting slaughtermen.
What say you? Will you yield, and this avoid?
Or, guilty in defence, be thus destroy'd?
   Gov. Our expectation hath this day an end.
The Dauphin, whom of succours we entreated,   45

Returns us that his powers are yet not ready
To raise so great a siege. Therefore, dread king,
We yield our town and lives to thy soft mercy.
Enter our gates, dispose of us and ours,
For we no longer are defensible.   50
   King. Open your gates.   [*Exit Governor.*]
                      Come, uncle Exeter,
Go you and enter Harflew; there remain
And fortify it strongly 'gainst the French.
Use mercy to them all. For us, dear uncle,
The winter coming on, and sickness growing   55
Upon our soldiers, we will retire to Calais.
To-night in Harflew will we be your guest;
To-morrow for the march are we addrest.
                 Flourish, and enter the town.

[Scene IV. *Rouen. The* French King's *Palace.*]

Enter *Katherine* and [*Alice*], an old *Gentlewoman.*

   Kath. Alice, tu as esté en Angleterre, et tu parles bien le
langage.
   Alice. Un peu, madame.
   Kath. Je te prie m'enseignez; il faut que j'apprenne à parler.
Comment appelez-vous la main en Anglois?   6
   Alice. La main? Elle est appelée 'de hand.'
   Kath. 'De hand.' Et les doigts?
   Alice. Les doigts? Ma foi, j'oublie les doigts; mais je me
souviendrai. Les doigts? Je pense qu'ils sont appelés 'de fin-
gres'; oui, 'de fingres.'   11
   Kath. La main, 'de hand'; les doigts, 'de fingres.' Je pense
que je suis le bon escolier; j'ai gagné deux mots d'Anglois
vistement. Comment appelez-vous les ongles?   15

Alice. Les ongles? Nous les appelons 'de nails.'

Kath. 'De nails.' Escoutez; dites-moi, si je parle bien: 'de hand, de fingres,' et 'de nails.'

Alice. C'est bien dict, madame; il est fort bon Anglois.   20

Kath. Dites-moi l'Anglois pour le bras.

Alice. 'De arm,' madame.

Kath. Et le coude.

Alice. 'D' elbow.'   24

Kath. 'D' elbow.' Je m'en fais la répétition de tous les mots que vous m'avez appris dès à présent.

Alice. Il est trop difficile, madame, comme je pense.   29

Kath. Excusez-moi, Alice; escoutez: 'd' hand, de fingres, de nails, d' arma, de bilbow.'

Alice. 'D' elbow,' madame.

Kath. O Seigneur Dieu, je m'en oublie! 'D' elbow.' Comment appelez-vous le col?

Alice. 'De nick,' madame.   35

Kath. 'De nick.' Et le menton?

Alice. 'De chin.'

Kath. 'De sin.' Le col, 'de nick'; le menton, 'de sin.'   39

Alice. Oui. Sauf vostre honneur, en vérité, vous prononcez les mots aussi droict que les natifs d'Angleterre.

Kath. Je ne doute point d'apprendre, par la grace de Dieu, et en peu de temps.   44

Alice. N'avez-vous pas déjà oublié ce que je vous ai enseigné?

Kath. Non, je réciterai à vous promptement: 'd' hand, de fingres, de mails'—

Alice. 'De nails,' madame.

Kath. 'De nails, de arm, de ilbow.'   50

Alice. Sauf vostre honneur, 'd' elbow.'

Kath. Ainsi dis-je; 'd' elbow, de nick,' et 'de sin.' Comment appelez-vous le pied et la robe?

Alice. 'De foot,' madame; et 'de coun.'   54

Kath. 'De foot et de coun!' O Seigneur Dieu! ce sont mots
de son mauvais, corruptible, gros, et impudique, et non pour
les dames d'honneur d'user: je ne voudrois prononcer ces mots
devant les seigneurs de France pour tout le monde. Foh! 'le
foot' et 'le coun'! Néantmoins, je réciterai une autre fois ma
leçon ensemble: 'd' hand, de fingres, de nails, d' arm, d' elbow,
de nick, de sin, de foot, de coun.'

Alice. Excellent, madame!   64

Kath. C'est assez pour une fois: allons-nous à diner. *Exeunt.*

[Scene V. *Rouen. The Palace.*]

Enter the *King of France*, the *Dauphin*, *Bourbon*, the *Constable
of France*, and others.

King. 'Tis certain he hath pass'd the river Somme.

Con. And if he be not fought withal, my lord,
Let us not live in France; let us quit all
And give our vineyards to a barbarous people.

Dau. O Dieu vivant! Shall a few sprays of us,   5
The emptying of our fathers' luxury,
Our scions, put in wild and savage stock,
Spirt up so suddenly into the clouds
And overlook their grafters?

Bour. Normans, but bastard Normans, Norman bastards! 10
Mort de ma vie! if they march along
Unfought withal, but I will sell my dukedom
To buy a slobb'ry and a dirty farm
In that nook-shotten isle of Albion.

Con. Dieu de batailles! whence have they this mettle?   15
Is not their climate foggy, raw, and dull,
On whom, as in despite, the sun looks pale,
Killing their fruit with frowns? Can sodden water,

A drench for sur-rein'd jades, their barley broth,
Decoct their cold blood to such valiant heat?   20
And shall our quick blood, spirited with wine,
Seem frosty? O, for honour of our land,
Let us not hang like roping icicles
Upon our houses' thatch, whiles a more frosty people
Sweat drops of gallant youth in our rich fields—   25
'Poor' we may call them in their native lords!
   Dau. By faith and honour,
Our madams mock at us and plainly say
Our mettle is bred out, and they will give
Their bodies to the lust of English youth   30
To new-store France with bastard warriors.
   Bour. They bid us to the English dancing schools
And teach lavoltas high and swift corantos,
Saying our grace is only in our heels
And that we are most lofty runaways.   35
   King. Where is Montjoy the herald? Speed him hence;
Let him greet England with our sharp defiance.
Up, princes! and, with spirit of honour edged,
More sharper than your swords, hie to the field.
Charles Delabreth, High Constable of France,   40
You Dukes of Orleans, Bourbon, and of Berri,
Alençon, Brabant, Bar, and Burgundy;
Jaques Chatillon, Rambures, Vaudemont,
Beaumont, Grandpré, Roussi, and Fauconberg,
Foix, Lestrale, Bouciqualt, and Charolois,   45
High dukes, great princes, barons, lords, and knights,
For your great seats now quit you of great shames.
Bar Harry England, that sweeps through our land
With pennons painted in the blood of Harflew.
Rush on his host as doth the melted snow   50
Upon the valleys whose low vassal seat

The Alps doth spit and void his rheum upon.
Go down upon him—you have power enough—
And in a captive chariot into Roan
Bring him our prisoner.
   Con.   This becomes the great.   55
Sorry am I his numbers are so few,
His soldiers sick and famish'd in their march;
For I am sure, when he shall see our army,
He'll drop his heart into the sink of fear
And, for achievement, offer us his ransom.   60
   King. Therefore, Lord Constable, haste on Montjoy,
And let him say to England that we send
To know what willing ransom he will give.
Prince Dauphin, you shall stay with us in Roan.
   Dau. Not so, I do beseech your Majesty.   65
   King. Be patient, for you shall remain with us.
Now forth, Lord Constable and princes all,
And quickly bring us word of England's fall.   *Exeunt.*

[Scene VI. *The English camp in Picardy.*]

Enter *Captains*, English and Welsh—*Gower* and *Fluellen.*

   Gow. How now, Captain Fluellen? Come you from the bridge?
   Flu. I assure you there is very excellent services committed at the bridge.
   Gow. Is the Duke of Exeter safe?   5
   Flu. The Duke of Exeter is as magnanimous as Agamemnon, and a man that I love and honour with my soul, and my heart, and my duty, and my live, and my living, and my uttermost power. He is not—God be praised and plessed!—any hurt in the world, but keeps the pridge most valiantly, with excellent

discipline. There is an aunchient lieutenant there at the pridge,
I think in my very conscience he is as valiant a man as Mark
Anthony, and he is a man of no estimation in the world, but I
did see him do as gallant service.

Gow. What do you call him?

Flu. He is call'd Aunchient Pistol.

Gow. I know him not.   20

Enter *Pistol*.

Flu. Here is the man.

Pist. Captain, I thee beseech to do me favours.
The Duke of Exeter doth love thee well.

Flu. Ay, I praise God; and I have merited some love at his
hands.   25

Pist. Bardolph, a soldier firm and sound of heart,
And of buxom valour, hath by cruel fate,
And giddy Fortune's furious fickle wheel—
That goddess blind,   30
That stands upon the rolling restless stone—

Flu. By your patience, Aunchient Pistol. Fortune is painted
plind, with a muffler afore her eyes, to signify to you that
Fortune is plind; and she is painted also with a wheel, to signify
to you, which is the moral of it, that she is turning and inconstant, and mutability, and variation; and her foot, look you,
is fixed upon a spherical stone, which rolls, and rolls, and rolls.
In good truth, the poet makes a most excellent description of it.
Fortune is an excellent moral.   40

Pist. Fortune is Bardolph's foe, and frowns on him;
For he hath stol'n a pax, and hanged must 'a be—
A damned death!
Let gallows gape for dog; let man go free,
And let not hemp his windpipe suffocate.   45
But Exeter hath given the doom of death

For pax of little price.
Therefore, go speak—the Duke will hear thy voice;
And let not Bardolph's vital thread be cut
With edge of penny cord and vile reproach.   50
Speak, Captain, for his life, and I will thee requite.

    Flu. Aunchient Pistol, I do partly understand your meaning.

    Pist. Why then, rejoice therefore!   54

    Flu. Certainly, aunchient, it is not a thing to rejoice at; for
if, look you, he were my brother, I would desire the Duke to use
his good pleasure and put him to execution; for discipline ought
to be used.

    Pist. Die and be damn'd! and figo for thy friendship!   60

    Flu. It is well.

    Pist. The fig of Spain!   *Exit.*

    Flu. Very good.

    Gow. Why, this is an arrant counterfeit rascal! I remember
him now—a bawd, a cutpurse.   65

    Flu. I'll assure you, 'a utt'red as prave words at the pridge
as you shall see in a summer's day. But it is very well. What he
has spoke to me, that is well, I warrant you, when time is serve.

    Gow. Why, 'tis a gull, a fool, a rogue, that now and then goes
to the wars to grace himself, at his return into London, under
the form of a soldier. And such fellows are perfect in the great
commanders' names, and they will learn you by rote where
services were done:—at such and such a sconce, at such a breach,
at such a convoy; who came off bravely, who was shot, who
disgrac'd, what terms the enemy stood on; and this they con
perfectly in the phrase of war, which they trick up with new-
tuned oaths; and what a beard of the General's cut and a horrid
suit of the camp will do among foaming bottles and ale-wash'd
wits is wonderful to be thought on. But you must learn to know
such slanders of the age, or else you may be marvellously
mistook.   85

Flu. I tell you what, Captain Gower, I do perceive he is not the man that he would gladly make show to the world he is. If I find a hole in his coat, I will tell him my mind. [*Drum within.*] Hark you, the King is coming, and I must speak with him from the pridge. 91

Drum and colours. Enter the *King* and his poor *Soldiers*, [and *Gloucester*].

God pless your Majesty!

King. How now, Fluellen? Cam'st thou from the bridge?

Flu. Ay, so please your Majesty. The Duke of Exeter has very gallantly maintain'd the pridge; the French is gone off, look you, and there is gallant and most prave passages. Marry, th' athversary was have possession of the pridge, but he is enforced to retire, and the Duke of Exeter is master of the pridge. I can tell your Majesty, the Duke is a prave man. 101

King. What men have you lost, Fluellen?

Flu. The perdition of th' athversary hath been very great, reasonable great. Marry, for my part, I think the Duke hath lost never a man but one that is like to be executed for robbing a church—one Bardolph, if your Majesty know the man. His face is all bubukles and whelks, and knobs, and flames o' fire, and his lips blows at his nose, and it is like a coal of fire, sometimes plue and sometimes red; but his nose is executed, and his fire's out.

King. We would have all such offenders so cut off. And we give express charge that in our marches through the country there be nothing compell'd from the villages, nothing taken but paid for; none of the French upbraided or abused in disdainful language; for when lenity and cruelty play for a kingdom, the gentler gamester is the soonest winner. 120

Tucket. Enter *Montjoy*.

Mont. You know me by my habit.

King. Well then, I know thee. What shall I know of thee?

Mont. My master's mind.

King. Unfold it.   124

Mont. Thus says my king:—Say thou to Harry of England:
Though we seem'd dead, we did but sleep. Advantage is a better
soldier than rashness. Tell him we could have rebuk'd him at
Harflew, but that we thought not good to bruise an injury till it
were full ripe. Now we speak upon our cue, and our voice is
imperial. England shall repent his folly, see his weakness, and
admire our sufferance. Bid him therefore consider of his ransom,
which must proportion the losses we have borne, the subjects
we have lost, the disgrace we have digested; which in weight
to re-answer, his pettiness would bow under. For our losses, his
exchequer is too poor; for th' effusion of our blood, the muster
of his kingdom too faint a number; and for our disgrace, his own
person kneeling at our feet but a weak and worthless satisfaction.
To this add defiance; and tell him for conclusion he hath be-
trayed his followers, whose condemnation is pronounc'd. So far
my king and master; so much my office.   145

King. What is thy name? I know thy quality.

Mont. Montjoy.

King. Thou dost thy office fairly. Turn thee back,
And tell thy king I do not seek him now,
But could be willing to march on to Calais   150
Without impeachment: for, to say the sooth,
Though 'tis no wisdom to confess so much
Unto an enemy of craft and vantage,
My people are with sickness much enfeebled,
My numbers lessen'd, and those few I have,   155
Almost no better than so many French;
Who when they were in health, I tell thee, herald,
I thought upon one pair of English legs
Did march three Frenchmen. Yet forgive me, God,
That I do brag thus! This your air of France   160

Hath blown that vice in me. I must repent.
Go therefore tell thy master here I am;
My ransom is this frail and worthless trunk;
My army but a weak and sickly guard;
Yet, God before, tell him we will come on,   165
Though France himself and such another neighbour
Stand in our way. There's for thy labour, Montjoy.

          [Gives a purse.]

Go bid thy master well advise himself:
If we may pass, we will; if we be hind'red,
We shall your tawny ground with your red **blood**   170
Discolour; and so, Montjoy, fare you well.
The sum of all our answer is but this:
We would not seek a battle, as we are,
Nor, as we are, we say we will not shun it.
So tell your master.   175
    Mont. I shall deliver so. Thanks to your Highness.   *[Exit.]*
    Glouc. I hope they will not come upon us now.
    King. We are in God's hand, brother, not in theirs.
March to the bridge. It now draws toward night.
Beyond the river we'll encamp ourselves,   180
And on to-morrow bid them march away.

          Exeunt.

[Scene VII. *The French camp, near Agincourt.*]

Enter the *Constable of France*, the *Lord Rambures*, *Orleans*,
Dauphin, with others.

    Con. Tut! I have the best armour of the world. Would it
were day!
    Orl. You have an excellent armour; but let my horse have
his due.

Con. It is the best horse of Europe.   5

Orl. Will it never be morning?

Dau. My Lord of Orleans, and my Lord High Constable,
you talk of horse and armour?

Orl. You are as well provided of both as any prince in the
world.   10

Dau. What a long night is this! I will not change my horse
with any that treads but on four pasterns. Ça, ha! he bounds
from the earth, as if his entrails were hairs; le cheval volant, the
Pegasus, avec les narines de feu! When I bestride him, I soar, I
am a hawk. He trots the air. The earth sings when he touches
it. The basest horn of his hoof is more musical than the pipe of
Hermes.

Orl. He's of the colour of the nutmeg.   20

Dau. And of the heat of the ginger. It is a beast for Perseus:
he is pure air and fire; and the dull elements of earth and water
never appear in him, but only in patient stillness while his rider
mounts him. He is indeed a horse, and all other jades you may
call beasts.   26

Con. Indeed, my lord, it is a most absolute and excellent
horse.

Dau. It is the prince of palfreys. His neigh is like the bidding
of a monarch, and his countenance enforces homage.   31

Orl. No more, cousin.

Dau. Nay, the man hath no wit that cannot, from the rising
of the lark to the lodging of the lamb, vary deserved praise on
my palfrey. It is a theme as fluent as the sea. Turn the sands
into eloquent tongues, and my horse is argument for them all.
'Tis a subject for a sovereign to reason on, and for a sovereign's
sovereign to ride on; and for the world, familiar to us and un-
known, to lay apart their particular functions and wonder at
him. I once writ a sonnet in his praise and began thus, 'Wonder
of nature!'

Orl. I have heard a sonnet begin so to one's mistress.   45

Dau. Then did they imitate that which I compos'd to my courser, for my horse is my mistress.

Orl. Your mistress bears well.

Dau. Me well, which is the prescript praise and perfection of a good and particular mistress.

Con. Nay, for methought yesterday your mistress shrewdly shook your back.

Dau. So perhaps did yours.

Con. Mine was not bridled.   54

Dau. O, then belike she was old and gentle, and you rode like a kern of Ireland, your French hose off, and in your strait strossers.

Con. You have good judgment in horsemanship.   59

Dau. Be warn'd by me then. They that ride so, and ride not warily, fall into foul bogs. I had rather have my horse to my mistress.

Con. I had as live have my mistress a jade.

Dau. I tell thee, Constable, my mistress wears his own hair.

Con. I could make as true a boast as that, if I had a sow to my mistress.

Dau. 'Le chien est retourné à son propre vomissement, et la truie lavée au bourbier.' Thou mak'st use of anything.   70

Con. Yet do I not use my horse for my mistress, or any such proverb so little kin to the purpose.

Ram. My Lord Constable, the armour that I saw in your tent to-night—are those stars or suns upon it?   75

Con. Stars, my lord.

Dau. Some of them will fall to-morrow, I hope.

Con. And yet my sky shall not want.

Dau. That may be, for you bear a many superfluously, and 'twere more honour some were away.   81

Con. Ev'n as your horse bears your praises, who would trot as well, were some of your brags dismounted.   84

Dau. Would I were able to load him with his desert! Will it never be day? I will trot to-morrow a mile, and my way shall be paved with English faces.

Con. I will not say so, for fear I should be fac'd out of my way; but I would it were morning, for I would fain be about the ears of the English. 92

Ram. Who will go to hazard with me for twenty prisoners?

Con. You must first go yourself to hazard ere you have them.

Dau. 'Tis midnight; I'll go arm myself. *Exit.* 97

Orl. The Dauphin longs for morning.

Ram. He longs to eat the English.

Con. I think he will eat all he kills. 100

Orl. By the white hand of my lady, he's a gallant prince.

Con. Swear by her foot, that she may tread out the oath.

Orl. He is simply the most active gentleman of France. 106

Con. Doing is activity, and he will still be doing.

Orl. He never did harm, that I heard of.

Con. Nor will do none to-morrow. He will keep that good name still. 111

Orl. I know him to be valiant.

Con. I was told that by one that knows him better than you.

Orl. What's he? 115

Con. Marry, he told me so himself, and he said he car'd not who knew it.

Orl. He needs not; it is no hidden virtue in him. 119

Con. By my faith, sir, but it is! Never anybody saw it but his lackey. 'Tis a hooded valour; and when it appears, it will bate.

Orl. Ill will never said well.

Con. I will cap that proverb with 'There is flattery in friendship.' 125

Orl. And I will take up that with 'Give the devil his due.'

Con. Well plac'd! There stands your friend for the devil. Have at the very eye of that proverb with 'A pox of the devil!'

Orl. You are the better at proverbs, by how much 'a fool's bolt is soon shot.'

Con. You have shot over.

Orl. 'Tis not the first time you were overshot.

Enter a *Messenger.*

Mess. My Lord High Constable, the English lie within fifteen hundred paces of your tents.

Con. Who hath measur'd the ground?

Mess. The Lord Grandpré. 138

Con. A valiant and most expert gentleman. Would it were day! Alas, poor Harry of England! He longs not for the dawning, as we do.

Orl. What a wretched and peevish fellow is this King of England, to mope with his fat-brain'd followers so far out of his knowledge!

Con. If the English had any apprehension, they would run away. 146

Orl. That they lack; for if their heads had any intellectual armour, they could never wear such heavy headpieces.

Ram. That island of England breeds very valiant creatures. Their mastiffs are of unmatchable courage. 152

Orl. Foolish curs, that run winking into the mouth of a Russian bear and have their heads crush'd like rotten apples! You may as well say that's a valiant flea that dare eat his breakfast on the lip of a lion. 157

Con. Just, just! and the men do sympathize with the mastiffs in robustious and rough coming on, leaving their wits with their wives; and then give them great meals of beef and iron and steel, they will eat like wolves and fight like devils. 162

Orl. Ay, but these English are shrowdly out of beef.

Con. Then shall we find to-morrow they have only stomachs to eat and none to fight. Now is it time to arm. Come, shall we about it?   167

Orl. It is now two o'clock; but let me see—by ten We shall have each a hundred Englishmen.

Exeunt.

Act [IV].

Chorus.

Now entertain conjecture of a time
When creeping murmur and the poring dark
Fills the wide vessel of the universe.
From camp to camp, through the foul womb of night,
The hum of either army stilly sounds,   5
That the fix'd sentinels almost receive
The secret whispers of each other's watch.
Fire answers fire, and through their paly flames
Each battle sees the other's umber'd face.
Steed threatens steed, in high and boastful neighs   10
Piercing the night's dull ear; and from the tents
The armourers accomplishing the knights,
With busy hammers closing rivets up,
Give dreadful note of preparation.
The country cocks do crow, the clocks do toll   15
And the third hour of drowsy morning name.
Proud of their numbers and secure in soul,
The confident and over-lusty French
Do the low-rated English play at dice;
And chide the cripple tardy-gaited night   20
Who like a foul and ugly witch doth limp
So tediously away. The poor condemned English,
Like sacrifices, by their watchful fires
Sit patiently and inly ruminate
The morning's danger; and their gesture sad,   25
Investing lank-lean cheeks and war-worn coats,
Presenteth them unto the gazing moon
So many horrid ghosts. O, now, who will behold
The royal captain of this ruin'd band
Walking from watch to watch, from tent to tent,   30

Let him cry 'Praise and glory on his head!'
For forth he goes and visits all his host,
Bids them good morrow with a modest smile
And calls them brothers, friends, and countrymen.
Upon his royal face there is no note   35
How dread an army hath enrounded him;
Nor doth he dedicate one jot of colour
Unto the weary and all-watched night,
But freshly looks, and overbears attaint
With cheerful semblance and sweet majesty;   40
That every wretch, pining and pale before,
Beholding him, plucks comfort from his looks.
A largess universal, like the sun,
His liberal eye doth give to every one,
Thawing cold fear. Then, mean and gentle all,   45
Behold, as may unworthiness define,
A little touch of Harry in the night.
And so our scene must to the battle fly;
Where (O for pity!) we shall much disgrace
With four or five most vile and ragged foils,   50
Right ill-dispos'd in brawl ridiculous,
The name of Agincourt. Yet sit and see,
Minding true things by what their mock'ries be.   *Exit.*

[Scene I. *France. The English camp at Agincourt.*]

Enter the *King*, *Bedford*, and *Gloucester*.

King. Gloucester, 'tis true that we are in great danger;
The greater therefore should our courage be.
Good morrow, brother Bedford. God Almighty!
There is some soul of goodness in things evil,
Would men observingly distil it out;   5

For our bad neighbour makes us early stirrers,
Which is both healthful, and good husbandry.
Besides, they are our outward consciences,
And preachers to us all, admonishing
That we should dress us fairly for our end.   10
Thus may we gather honey from the weed
And make a moral of the devil himself.

                    Enter *Erpingham.*

Good morrow, old Sir Thomas Erpingham.
A good soft pillow for that good white head
Were better than a churlish turf of France.   15
    Erp. Not so, my liege. This lodging likes me better,
Since I may say 'Now lie I like a king.'
    King. 'Tis good for men to love their present pains
Upon example: so the spirit is eas'd;
And when the mind is quick'ned, out of doubt   20
The organs, though defunct and dead before,
Break up their drowsy grave and newly move
With casted slough and fresh legerity.
Lend me thy cloak, Sir Thomas. Brothers both,
Commend me to the princes in our camp;   25
Do my good morrow to them, and anon
Desire them all to my pavilion.
    Glouc. We shall, my liege.
    Erp. Shall I attend your Grace?
    King.   No, my good knight.
Go with my brothers to my lords of England.   30
I and my bosom must debate awhile,
And then I would no other company.
    Erp. The Lord in heaven bless thee, noble Harry!
                              Exeunt [*all but the King*].
    King. God-a-mercy, old heart! thou speak'st cheerfully.

Enter *Pistol*.

Pist. Qui va là?   35
King. A friend.
Pist. Discuss unto me, art thou officer;
Or art thou base, common, and popular?
King. I am a gentleman of a company.
Pist. Trail'st thou the puissant pike?   40
King. Even so. What are you?
Pist. As good a gentleman as the Emperor.
King. Then you are a better than the King.
Pist. The King's a bawcock, and a heart of gold,
A lad of life, an imp of fame,   45
Of parents good, of fist most valiant.
I kiss his dirty shoe, and from heartstring
I love the lovely bully. What is thy name?
King. Harry le Roy.
Pist. Le Roy? A Cornish name. Art thou of Cornish
    crew?   50
King. No, I am a Welshman.
Pist. Know'st thou Fluellen?
King. Yes.
Pist. Tell him I'll knock his leek about his pate
Upon Saint Davy's day.   55
King. Do not you wear your dagger in your cap that day,
lest he knock that about yours.
Pist. Art thou his friend?
King. And his kinsman too.
Pist. The figo for thee then!   60
King. I thank you. God be with you!
Pist. My name is Pistol call'd.

                                                Exit. Manet King.
King. It sorts well with your fierceness.

Enter *Fluellen* and *Gower*.

Gow. Captain Fluellen!   64

Flu. So! in the name of Jesu Christ, speak lower. It is the
greatest admiration in the universal world, when the true and
aunchient prerogatifes and laws of the wars is not kept. If you
would take the pains but to examine the wars of Pompey the
Great, you shall find, I warrant you, that there is no tiddle
taddle nor pibble pabble in Pompey's camp. I warrant you,
you shall find the ceremonies of the wars, and the cares of it,
and the forms of it, and the sobriety of it, and the modesty of
it, to be otherwise.   75

Gow. Why, the enemy is loud; you hear him all night.

Flu. If the enemy is an ass and a fool and a prating coxcomb,
is it meet, think you, that we should also, look you, be an ass
and a fool and a prating coxcomb? In your own conscience now?

Gow. I will speak lower.

Flu. I pray you and beseech you that you will.

Exeunt [*Gower and Fluellen*].

King. Though it appear a little out of fashion,   85
There is much care and valour in this Welshman.

Enter three Soldiers, *John Bates*, *Alexander Court*,
and *Michael Williams*.

Court. Brother John Bates, is not that the morning which
breaks yonder?

Bates. I think it be; but we have no great cause to desire the
approach of day.   90

Will. We see yonder the beginning of the day, but I think
we shall never see the end of it. Who goes there?

King. A friend.

Will. Under what captain serve you?   95

King. Under Sir Thomas Erpingham.

Will. A good old commander and a most kind gentleman. I
pray you, what thinks he of our estate?   99

King. Even as men wrack'd upon a sand, that look to be
wash'd off the next tide.

Bates. He hath not told his thought to the King?

King. No; nor is it not meet he should. For though I speak
it to you, I think the King is but a man, as I am. The violet
smells to him as it doth to me; the element shows to him as it
doth to me; all his senses have but human conditions. His
ceremonies laid by, in his nakedness he appears but a man; and
though his affections are higher mounted than ours, yet, when
they stoop, they stoop with the like wing. Therefore, when he
sees reason of fears, as we do, his fears, out of doubt, be of the
same relish as ours are. Yet, in reason, no man should possess
him with any appearance of fear, lest he, by showing it, should
dishearten his army.   117

Bates. He may show what outward courage he will; but I
believe, as cold a night as 'tis, he could wish himself in Thames
up to the neck; and so I would he were, and I by him, at all
adventures, so we were quit here.   122

King. By my troth, I will speak my conscience of the King:
I think he would not wish himself anywhere but where he is.

Bates. Then I would he were here alone. So should he be
sure to be ransomed, and a many poor men's lives saved. ⟨128⟩

King. I dare say you love him not so ill to wish him here
alone, howsoever you speak this to feel other men's minds. Methinks I could not die anywhere so contented as in the King's
company, his cause being just and his quarrel honourable.

Will. That's more than we know.   135

Bates. Ay, or more than we should seek after; for we know
enough if we know we are the King's subjects. If his cause be
wrong, our obedience to the King wipes the crime of it out of us.

Will. But if the cause be not good, the King himself hath a

heavy reckoning to make when all those legs and arms and
heads, chopp'd off in a battle, shall join together at the latter
day and cry all 'We died at such a place!' some swearing, some
crying for a surgeon, some upon their wives left poor behind
them, some upon the debts they owe, some upon their children
rawly left. I am afeard there are few die well that die in a
battle; for how can they charitably dispose of anything when
blood is their argument? Now, if these men do not die well, it
will be a black matter for the King that led them to it; who to
disobey were against all proportion of subjection. 153

King. So, if a son that is by his father sent about merchandise
do sinfully miscarry upon the sea, the imputation of his wickedness, by your rule, should be imposed upon his father that
sent him; or if a servant, under his master's command trans-
porting a sum of money, be assailed by robbers and die in many
irreconcil'd iniquities, you may call the business of the master
the author of the servant's damnation. But this is not so. The
King is not bound to answer the particular endings of his soldiers, the father of his son, nor the master of his servant; for
they purpose not their death when they purpose their services.
Besides, there is no king, be his cause never so spotless, if it
come to the arbitrement of swords, can try it out with all unspotted soldiers. Some (peradventure) have on them the guilt
of premeditated and contrived murther; some, of beguiling virgins with the broken seals of perjury; some, making the wars
their bulwark, that have before gored the gentle bosom of
peace with pillage and robbery. Now, if these men have de-
feated the law and outrun native punishment, though they can
outstrip men, they have no wings to fly from God. War is his
beadle, war is his vengeance; so that here men are punish'd for
before-breach of the King's laws in now the King's quarrel.
Where they feared the death, they have borne life away; and
where they would be safe, they perish. Then if they die un-

provided, no more is the King guilty of their damnation than
he was before guilty of those impieties for the which they are
now visited. Every subject's duty is the King's, but every
subject's soul is his own. Therefore should every soldier in the
wars do as every sick man in his bed—wash every mote out of
his conscience; and dying so, death is to him advantage; or
not dying, the time was blessedly lost wherein such preparation
was gained; and in him that escapes, it were not sin to think
that, making God so free an offer, he let him outlive that day
to see his greatness and to teach others how they should prepare.

Will. 'Tis certain, every man that dies ill, the ill upon his
own head—the King is not to answer it.

Bates. I do not desire he should answer for me, and yet I
determine to fight lustily for him.

King. I myself heard the King say he would not be ransom'd. 203

Will. Ay, he said so, to make us fight cheerfully; but when
our throats are cut, he may be ransom'd, and we ne'er the wiser.

King. If I live to see it, I will never trust his word after. 208

Will. You pay him then! That's a perilous shot out of an
elder-gun that a poor and a private displeasure can do against
a monarch! You may as well go about to turn the sun to ice
with fanning in his face with a peacock's feather. You'll never
trust his word after! Come, 'tis a foolish saying. 215

King. Your reproof is something too round. I should be angry
with you if the time were convenient.

Will. Let it be a quarrel between us if you live. 220

King. I embrace it.

Will. How shall I know thee again?

King. Give me any gage of thine, and I will wear it in my
bonnet. Then, if ever thou dar'st acknowledge it, I will make it
my quarrel.

Will. Here's my glove. Give me another of thine. 227

King. There.

Will. This will I also wear in my cap. If ever thou come to
me and say, after to-morrow, 'This is my glove,' by this hand, I
will take thee a box on the ear.   232

King. If ever I live to see it, I will challenge it.

Will. Thou dar'st as well be hang'd.

King. Well, I will do it, though I take thee in the King's
company.

Will. Keep thy word. Fare thee well.

Bates. Be friends, you English fools, be friends! We have
French quarrels enow, if you could tell how to reckon.   241

King. Indeed the French may lay twenty French crowns to
one they will beat us, for they bear them on their shoulders;
but it is no English treason to cut French crowns, and to-
morrow the King himself will be a clipper.   246

                                                 Exeunt Soldiers.

Upon the King! Let us our lives, our souls,
Our debts, our careful wives,
Our children, and our sins, lay on the King!
We must bear all. O hard condition,   250
Twin-born with greatness, subject to the breath
Of every fool, whose sense no more can feel
But his own wringing! What infinite heart's-ease
Must kings neglect that private men enjoy!
And what have kings that privates have not too,   255
Save ceremony, save general ceremony?
And what art thou, thou idol Ceremony?
What kind of god art thou, that suffer'st more
Of mortal griefs than do thy worshippers?
What are thy rents? What are thy comings-in?   260
O Ceremony, show me but thy worth!
What is thy soul of adoration?
Art thou aught else but place, degree, and form,

Creating awe and fear in other men?
Wherein thou art less happy being fear'd   265
Than they in fearing.
What drink'st thou oft, instead of homage sweet,
But poison'd flattery? O, be sick, great greatness,
And bid thy ceremony give thee cure!
Think'st thou the fiery fever will go out   270
With titles blown from adulation?
Will it give place to flexure and low bending?
Canst thou, when thou command'st the beggar's knee,
Command the health of it? No, thou proud dream,
That play'st so subtilly with a king's repose.   275
I am a king that find thee; and I know
'Tis not the balm, the sceptre, and the ball,
The sword, the mace, the crown imperial,
The intertissued robe of gold and pearl,
The farced title running fore the king,   280
The throne he sits on, nor the tide of pomp
That beats upon the high shore of this world—
No, not all these, thrice-gorgeous ceremony,
Not all these, laid in bed majestical,
Can sleep so soundly as the wretched slave,   285
Who, with a body fill'd, and vacant mind,
Gets him to rest, cramm'd with distressful bread;
Never sees horrid night, the child of hell;
But like a lackey, from the rise to set,
Sweats in the eye of Phœbus, and all night   290
Sleeps in Elysium; next day after dawn,
Doth rise and help Hyperion to his horse;
And follows so the ever-running year
With profitable labour to his grave;
And but for ceremony, such a wretch,   295
Winding up days with toil and nights with sleep,

Had the forehand and vantage of a king.
The slave, a member of the country's peace,
Enjoys it; but in gross brain little wots
What watch the king keeps to maintain the peace,   300
Whose hours the peasant best advantages.

Enter *Erpingham.*

   Erp. My lord, your nobles, jealous of your absence,
Seek through your camp to find you.
   King.   Good old knight,
Collect them all together at my tent.
I'll be before thee.
    Erp.   I shall do't, my lord.   *Exit.* 305
   King. O God of battles, steel my soldiers' hearts,
Possess them not with fear! Take from them now
The sense of reck'ning, if th' opposed numbers
Pluck their hearts from them. Not to-day, O Lord,
O, not to-day, think not upon the fault   310
My father made in compassing the crown!
I Richard's body have interred new;
And on it have bestowed more contrite tears
Than from it issued forced drops of blood.
Five hundred poor I have in yearly pay,   315
Who twice a day their wither'd hands hold up
Toward heaven, to pardon blood; and I have built
Two chantries, where the sad and solemn priests
Sing still for Richard's soul. More will I do!
Though all that I can do is nothing worth,   320
Since that my penitence comes after all,
Imploring pardon.

Enter *Gloucester.*

   Glouc. My liege!
   King. My brother Gloucester's voice. Ay.

I know thy errand; I will go with thee.   325
The day, my friends, and all things stay for me.   *Exeunt.*

[Scene II. *The French camp.*]

Enter the *Dauphin, Orleans, Rambures,* and *Beaumont.*

Orl. The sun doth gild our armour. Up, my lords!
Dau. Montez à cheval! My horse! Varlet, laquais! Ha!
Orl. O brave spirit!
Dau. Via! les eaux et la terre—
Orl. Rien puis? L'air et le feu.   5
Dau. Ciel! cousin Orleans.

Enter *Constable.*

Now, my Lord Constable?
   Con. Hark how our steeds for present service neigh!
   Dau. Mount them and make incision in their hides,
That their hot blood may spin in English eyes   10
And dout them with superfluous courage, ha!
   Ram. What, will you have them weep our horses' blood?
How shall we then behold their natural tears?

Enter *Messenger.*

   Mess. The English are embattail'd, you French peers.
   Con. To horse, you gallant princes! straight to horse!   15
Do but behold yond poor and starved band,
And your fair show shall suck away their souls,
Leaving them but the shales and husks of men.
There is not work enough for all our hands,
Scarce blood enough in all their sickly veins   20
To give each naked curtleaxe a stain
That our French gallants shall to-day draw out

And sheathe for lack of sport. Let us but blow on them,
The vapour of our valour will o'erturn them.
'Tis positive 'gainst all exceptions, lords,   25
That our superfluous lackeys and our peasants,
Who in unnecessary action swarm
About our squares of battle, were enow
To purge this field of such a hilding foe,
Though we upon this mountain's basis by   30
Took stand for idle speculation:
But that our honours must not. What's to say?
A very little little let us do,
And all is done. Then let the trumpets sound
The tucket sonance and the note to mount;   35
For our approach shall so much dare the field
That England shall couch down in fear and yield.

Enter *Grandpré*.

   Grand. Why do you stay so long, my lords of France?
Yond island carrions, desperate of their bones,
Ill-favouredly become the morning field.   40
Their ragged curtains poorly are let loose,
And our air shakes them passing scornfully.
Big Mars seems bankrout in their beggar'd host
And faintly through a rusty beaver peeps.
The horsemen sit like fixed candlesticks   45
With torch-staves in their hand; and their poor jades
Lob down their heads, dropping the hides and hips,
The gum down roping from their pale-dead eyes,
And in their pale dull mouths the gimmal'd bit
Lies foul with chaw'd grass, still and motionless;   50
And their executors, the knavish crows,
Fly o'er them, all impatient for their hour.
Description cannot suit itself in words

To demonstrate the life of such a battle
In life so liveless as it shows itself.   55
  Con. They have said their prayers, and they stay for death.
  Dau. Shall we go send them dinners and fresh suits
And give their fasting horses provender,
And after fight with them?
  Con. I stay but for my guidon. To the field!   60
I will the banner from a trumpet take
And use it for my haste. Come, come away!
The sun is high, and we outwear the day.   *Exeunt.*

[Scene III. *The English camp.*]

Enter *Gloucester, Bedford, Exeter, Erpingham* with all his host,
    Salisbury, and *Westmoreland*.

  Glouc. Where is the King?
  Bed. The King himself is rode to view their battle.
  West. Of fighting men they have full three-score thousand.
  Exe. There's five to one; besides, they all are fresh.
  Sal. God's arm strike with us! 'Tis a fearful odds.   5
God b' wi' you, princes all; I'll to my charge.
If we no more meet till we meet in heaven,
Then joyfully, my noble Lord of Bedford,
My dear Lord Gloucester, and my good Lord Exeter,
And my kind kinsman, warriors all, adieu!   10
  Bed. Farewell, good Salisbury, and good luck go with thee!
  Exe. Farewell, kind lord. Fight valiantly to-day;
And yet I do thee wrong to mind thee of it,
For thou art fram'd of the firm truth of valour.
                  [*Exit Salisbury.*]
  Bed. He is as full of valour as of kindness,   15
Princely in both.

Enter the *King*.

　West.　　　　　O that we now had here
But one ten thousand of those men in England
That do no work to-day!
　King.　　　　　　　What's he that wishes so?
My cousin Westmoreland? No, my fair cousin.
If we are mark'd to die, we are enow　　　　　　20
To do our country loss; and if to live,
The fewer men, the greater share of honour.
God's will! I pray thee wish not one man more.
By Jove, I am not covetous for gold,
Nor care I who doth feed upon my cost;　　　　25
It yearns me not if men my garments wear;
Such outward things dwell not in my desires:
But if it be a sin to covet honour,
I am the most offending soul alive.
No, faith, my coz, wish not a man from England.　30
God's peace! I would not lose so great an honour
As one man more methinks would share from me
For the best hope I have. O, do not wish one more!
Rather proclaim it, Westmoreland, through my host,
That he which hath no stomach to this fight,　　35
Let him depart; his passport shall be made,
And crowns for convoy put into his purse.
We would not die in that man's company
That fears his fellowship to die with us.
This day is call'd the Feast of Crispian.　　　40
He that outlives this day, and comes safe home,
Will stand a-tiptoe when this day is nam'd
And rouse him at the name of Crispian.
He that shall live this day, and see old age,
Will yearly on the vigil feast his neighbours　　45

And say 'To-morrow is Saint Crispian.'
Then will he strip his sleeve and show his scars,
And say 'These wounds I had on Crispin's day.'
Old men forget; yet all shall be forgot,
But he'll remember, with advantages,   50
What feats he did that day. Then shall our names,
Familiar in his mouth as household words—
Harry the King, Bedford and Exeter,
Warwick and Talbot, Salisbury and Gloucester—
Be in their flowing cups freshly rememb'red.   55
This story shall the good man teach his son;
And Crispin Crispian shall ne'er go by,
From this day to the ending of the world,
But we in it shall be remembered—
We few, we happy few, we band of brothers;   60
For he to-day that sheds his blood with me
Shall be my brother. Be he ne'er so vile,
This day shall gentle his condition;
And gentlemen in England now abed
Shall think themselves accurs'd they were not here,   65
And hold their manhoods cheap whiles any speaks
That fought with us upon Saint Crispin's day.

Enter Salisbury.

  Sal. My sovereign lord, bestow yourself with speed.
The French are bravely in their battles set
And will with all expedience charge on us.   70
  King. All things are ready, if our minds be so.
  West. Perish the man whose mind is backward now!
  King. Thou dost not wish more help from England, coz?
  West. God's will, my liege! would you and I alone,
Without more help, could fight this royal battle!   75
  King. Why, now thou hast unwish'd five thousand men!

Which likes me better than to wish us one.
You know your places. God be with you all!

Tucket. Enter *Montjoy.*

Mont. Once more I come to know of thee, King Harry,
If for thy ransom thou wilt now compound,   80
Before thy most assured overthrow;
For certainly thou art so near the gulf
Thou needs must be englutted. Besides, in mercy,
The Constable desires thee thou wilt mind
Thy followers of repentance, that their souls   85
May make a peaceful and a sweet retire
From all these fields, where (wretches!) their poor bodies
Must lie and fester.
    King.   Who hath sent thee now?
    Mont. The Constable of France.
    King. I pray thee bear my former answer back: 90
Bid them achieve me, and then sell my bones.
Good God! why should they mock poor fellows thus?
The man that once did sell the lion's skin
While the beast liv'd, was kill'd with hunting him.
A many of our bodies shall no doubt   95
Find native graves; upon the which, I trust,
Shall witness live in brass of this day's work;
And those that leave their valiant bones in France,
Dying like men, though buried in your dunghills,
They shall be fam'd; for there the sun shall greet them   100
And draw their honours reeking up to heaven,
Leaving their earthly parts to choke your clime,
The smell whereof shall breed a plague in France.
Mark then abounding valour in our English,
That, being dead, like to the bullet's grazing,   105
Break out into a second course of mischief,

Killing in relapse of mortality.
Let me speak proudly. Tell the Constable
We are but warriors for the working day.
Our gayness and our gilt are all besmirch'd   110
With rainy marching in the painful field.
There's not a piece of feather in our host—
Good argument, I hope, we will not fly—
And time hath worn us into slovenry.
But, by the mass, our hearts are in the trim;   115
And my poor soldiers tell me, yet ere night
They'll be in fresher robes, or they will pluck
The gay new coats o'er the French soldiers' heads
And turn them out of service. If they do this
(As, if God please, they shall), my ransom then   120
Will soon be levied. Herald, save thou thy labour.
Come thou no more for ransom, gentle herald.
They shall have none, I swear, but these my joints;
Which if they have as I will leave 'em them,
Shall yield them little, tell the Constable.   125
    Mont. I shall, King Harry. And so fare thee well.
Thou never shalt hear herald any more.   *Exit.*
    King. I fear thou wilt once more come again for ransom.

Enter *York.*

    York. My lord, most humbly on my knee I beg
The leading of the vaward.   130
    King. Take it, brave York. Now, soldiers, march away;
And how thou pleasest, God, dispose the day!
                    Exeunt.

[Scene IV. *The field of battle.*]

Alarum. Excursions. Enter *Pistol, French Soldier, Boy.*

Pist. Yield, cur!

French. Je pense que vous estes le gentilhomme de bonne
qualité.

Pist. Quality! Callino custore me! Art thou a gentleman?
What is thy name? Discuss. 5

French. O Seigneur Dieu!

Pist. O Signieur Dew should be a gentleman.
Perpend my words, O Signieur Dew, and mark.
O Signieur Dew, thou diest on point of fox,
Except, O signieur, thou do give to me 10
Egregious ransom.

French. O, prenez miséricorde! ayez pitié de moi!

Pist. Moy shall not serve. I will have forty moys;
Or I will fetch thy rim out at thy throat 15
In drops of crimson blood.

French. Est-il impossible d'eschapper la force de ton bras?

Pist. Brass, cur?
Thou damned and luxurious mountain goat, 20
Offer'st me brass?

French. O, pardonnez-moi!

Pist. Say'st thou me so? Is that a ton of moys?
Come hither, boy; ask me this slave in French
What is his name. 25

Boy. Escoutez. Comment estes-vous appelé?

French. Monsieur le Fer.

Boy. He says his name is Master Fer.

Pist. Master Fer? I'll fer him, and firk him, and ferret him!
Discuss the same in French unto him. 31

Boy. I do not know the French for 'fer,' and 'ferret,' and
'firk.'

Pist. Bid him prepare, for I will cut his throat.

French. Que dit-il, monsieur?   35

Boy. Il me commande à vous dire que vous faites vous prest;
car ce soldat ici est disposé tout à cette heure de couper vostre
gorge.

Pist. Owy, cuppele gorge, permafoy!

Peasant, unless thou give me crowns, brave crowns;   40
Or mangled shalt thou be by this my sword.

French. O, je vous supplie, pour l'amour de Dieu, me pardonner! Je suis gentilhomme de bonne maison. Gardez ma vie,
et je vous donnerai deux cents escus.   45

Pist. What are his words?

Boy. He prays you to save his life. He is a gentleman of a
good house, and for his ransom he will give you two hundred
crowns.

Pist. Tell him my fury shall abate, and I   50
The crowns will take.

French. Petit monsieur, que dit-il?

Boy. Encore qu'il est contre son jurement de pardonner
aucun prisonnier, néantmoins, pour les escus que vous l'avez
promis, il est content de vous donner la liberté, le franchisement.

French. Sur mes genoux je vous donne mille remercîmens; et
je m'estime heureux que je suis tombé entre les mains d'un
chevalier, je pense, le plus brave, vaillant, et très-distingué
seigneur d'Angleterre.   61

Pist. Expound unto me, boy.

Boy. He gives you, upon his knees, a thousand thanks; and
he esteems himself happy that he hath fall'n into the hands of
one (as he thinks) the most brave, valorous, and thrice-worthy
signieur of England.   67

Pist. As I suck blood, I will some mercy show!
Follow me, cur.   [*Exit.*]

Boy. Suivez-vous le grand Capitaine. [*Exit French Soldier.*]

I did never know so full a voice issue from so empty a heart;
but the saying is true, 'The empty vessel makes the greatest
sound.' Bardolph and Nym had ten times more valour than
this roaring devil i' th' old play that every one may pare his
nails with a wooden dagger; and they are both hang'd; and so
would this be, if he durst steal anything adventurously. I must
stay with the lackeys with the luggage of our camp. The French
might have a good prey of us, if he knew of it; for there is none
to guard it but boys.   *Exit.*

[Scene V. *Another part of the field of battle.*]

Enter *Constable, Orleans, Bourbon, Dauphin,* and *Rambures.*

Con. O diable!

Orl. O Seigneur! le jour est perdu, tout est perdu!

Dau. Mort de ma vie! all is confounded, all!
Reproach and everlasting shame   4
Sits mocking in our plumes.

                                                A short alarum.

O méchante fortune! Do not run away.

Con. Why, all our ranks are broke.

Dau. O perdurable shame! Let's stab ourselves.
Be these the wretches that we play'd at dice for?

Orl. Is this the king we sent to for his ransom?

Bour. Shame, and eternal shame! nothing but shame!   10
Let's die in honour. Once more back again!
And he that will not follow Bourbon now,
Let him go hence, and with his cap in hand
Like a base pander hold the chamber door
Whilst by a slave, no gentler than my dog,   15
His fairest daughter is contaminated.

Con. Disorder, that hath spoil'd us, friend us now!
Let us on heaps go offer up our lives.

Orl. We are enow yet living in the field
To smother up the English in our throngs,   20
If any order might be thought upon.
    Bour. The devil take order now! I'll to the throng.
Let life be short; else shame will be too long.

                                   Exeunt.

          [Scene VI. *Another part of the field.*]

Alarum. Enter the *King* and his *Train*, [*Exeter*, and others,]
                  with *Prisoners*.

    King. Well have we done, thrice-valiant countrymen;
But all's not done, yet keep the French the field.
    Exe. The Duke of York commends him to your Majesty.
    King. Lives he, good uncle? Thrice within this hour
I saw him down; thrice up again and fighting.   5
From helmet to the spur all blood he was.
    Exe. In which array, brave soldier, doth he lie,
Larding the plain; and by his bloody side,
Yoke-fellow to his honour-owing wounds,
The noble Earl of Suffolk also lies.   10
Suffolk first died; and York, all haggled over,
Comes to him, where in gore he lay insteep'd,
And takes him by the beard, kisses the gashes
That bloodily did yawn upon his face,
And cries aloud, 'Tarry, dear cousin Suffolk!   15
My soul shall thine keep company to heaven.
Tarry, sweet soul, for mine, then fly abreast;
As in this glorious and well-foughten field
We kept together in our chivalry!'
Upon these words I came and cheer'd him up.   20
He smil'd me in the face, raught me his hand,
And, with a feeble gripe, says 'Dear my lord,

Commend my service to my sovereign.'
So did he turn, and over Suffolk's neck
He threw his wounded arm and kiss'd his lips;   25
And so, espous'd to death, with blood he seal'd
A testament of noble-ending love.
The pretty and sweet manner of it forc'd
Those waters from me which I would have stopp'd;
But I had not so much of man in me,   30
And all my mother came into mine eyes
And gave me up to tears.
  King.   I blame you not;
For, hearing this, I must perforce compound
With mistful eyes, or they will issue too.

                                        Alarum.

But hark! what new alarum is this same?   35
The French have reinforc'd their scatter'd men.
Then every soldier kill his prisoners!
Give the word through.   *Exeunt.*

[Scene VII. *Another part of the field.*]

Enter *Fluellen* and *Gower.*

  Flu. Kill the poys and the luggage? 'Tis expressly against
the law of arms. 'Tis as arrant a piece of knavery, mark you
now, as can be offert. In your conscience, now, is it not?   4
  Gow. 'Tis certain there's not a boy left alive; and the cowardly rascals that ran from the battle ha' done this slaughter.
Besides, they have burned and carried away all that was in the
King's tent; wherefore the King most worthily hath caus'd
every soldier to cut his prisoner's throat. O, 'tis a gallant king!   11
  Flu. Ay, he was porn at Monmouth, Captain Gower. What
call you the town's name where Alexander the Pig was born?
  Gow. Alexander the Great.   15

Flu. Why, I pray you, is not 'pig' great? The pig, or the great, or the mighty, or the huge, or the magnanimous are all one reckonings, save the phrase is a little variations.

Gow. I think Alexander the Great was born in Macedon. His father was called Philip of Macedon, as I take it.   22

Flu. I think it is in Macedon where Alexander is porn. I tell you, Captain, if you look in the maps of the orld, I warrant you sall find, in the comparisons between Macedon and Monmouth, that the situations, look you, is both alike. There is a river in Macedon, and there is also moreover a river at Monmouth. It is call'd Wye at Monmouth; but it is out of my prains what is the name of the other river. But 'tis all one; 'tis alike as my fingers is to my fingers, and there is salmons in both. If you mark Alexander's life well, Harry of Monmouth's life is come after it indifferent well; for there is figures in all things. Alexander, God knows and you know, in his rages, and his furies, and his wraths, and his cholers, and his moods, and his displeasures, and his indignations, and also being a little intoxicates in his prains, did, in his ales and his angers, look you, kill his best friend, Cleitus.   41

Gow. Our King is not like him in that. He never kill'd any of his friends.

Flu. It is not well done, mark you now, to take the tales out of my mouth ere it is made and finished. I speak but in the figures and comparisons of it. As Alexander kill'd his friend Cleitus, being in his ales and his cups, so also Harry Monmouth, being in his right wits and his good judgments, turn'd away the fat knight with the great belly doublet. He was full of jests, and gipes, and knaveries, and mocks. I have forgot his name.

Gow. Sir John Falstaff.   54

Flu. That is he. I'll tell you there is good men porn at Monmouth.

Gow. Here comes his Majesty.

Alarum. Enter *King Harry*, [*Warwick, Gloucester, Exeter,*
        and others,] with *Prisoners. Flourish.*

King. I was not angry since I came to France
Until this instant. Take a trumpet, herald;
Ride thou unto the horsemen on yond hill.   60
If they will fight with us, bid them come down,
Or void the field. They do offend our sight.
If they'll do neither, we will come to them
And make them skirr away as swift as stones
Enforced from the old Assyrian slings.   65
Besides, we'll cut the throats of those we have;
And not a man of them that we shall take
Shall taste our mercy. Go and tell them so.

            Enter *Montjoy* [the *Herald*].

Exe. Here comes the herald of the French, my liege.
Glouc. His eyes are humbler than they us'd to be.   70
King. How now? What means this, herald? Know'st thou not
That I have fin'd these bones of mine for ransom?
Com'st thou again for ransom?
Herald.   No, great King.
I come to thee for charitable license
That we may wander o'er this bloody field   75
To look our dead, and then to bury them;
To sort our nobles from our common men;
For many of our princes (woe the while!)
Lie drown'd and soak'd in mercenary blood;
So do our vulgar drench their peasant limbs   80
In blood of princes; and the wounded steeds
Fret fetlock-deep in gore and with wild rage
Yerk out their armed heels at their dead masters,
Killing them twice. O, give us leave, great King,
To view the field in safety and dispose   85

Of their dead bodies!

King.   I tell thee truly, herald,
I know not if the day be ours or no;
For yet a many of your horsemen peer
And gallop o'er the field.

Herald.   The day is yours.

King. Praised be God and not our strength for it!   90
What is this castle call'd that stands hard by?

Herald. They call it Agincourt.

King. Then call we this the field of Agincourt,
Fought on the day of Crispin Crispianus.   94

Flu. Your grandfather of famous memory, an't please your
Majesty, and your great-uncle Edward the Plack Prince of
Wales, as I have read in the chronicles, fought a most prave
pattle here in France.

King. They did, Fluellen.   100

Flu. Your Majesty says very true. If your Majesties is re-
mem'bred of it, the Welshmen did good service in a garden
where leeks did grow, wearing leeks in their Monmouth caps;
which your Majesty know to this hour is an honourable badge
of the service; and I do believe your Majesty takes no scorn
to wear the leek upon Saint Tavy's day.   108

King. I wear it for a memorable honour;
For I am Welsh, you know, good countryman.

Flu. All the water in Wye cannot wash your Majesty's Welsh
plood out of your pody, I can tell you that. God pless it and
preserve it, as long as it pleases his grace, and his majesty too!

King. Thanks, good my countryman.   115

Flu. By Jeshu, I am your Majesty's countryman, I care not
who know it! I will confess it to all the orld. I need not to be
ashamed of your Majesty, praised be God, so long as your
Majesty is an honest man.   120

King. God keep me so!

Enter *Williams*.

Our heralds go with him.
Bring me just notice of the numbers dead
On both our parts.

[*Exeunt Heralds with Montjoy.*]
Call yonder fellow hither.

Exe. Soldier, you must come to the King.

King. Soldier, why wear'st thou that glove in thy cap?

Will. An't please your Majesty, 'tis the gage of one that I should fight withal, if he be alive.

King. An Englishman? 129

Will. An't please your Majesty, a rascal that swagger'd with me last night; who, if 'a live and ever dare to challenge this glove, I have sworn to take him a box o' th' ear; or if I can see my glove in his cap, which he swore, as he was a soldier, he would wear (if alive), I will strike it out soundly. 136

King. What think you, Captain Fluellen? Is it fit this soldier keep his oath?

Flu. He is a craven and a villain else, an't please your Majesty, in my conscience. 140

King. It may be his enemy is a gentleman of great sort, quite from the answer of his degree.

Flu. Though he be as good a gentleman as the devil is, as Lucifer and Belzebub himself, it is necessary, look your Grace, that he keep his vow and his oath. If he be perjur'd, see you now, his reputation is as arrant a villain and a Jacksauce as ever his black shoe trod upon God's ground and his earth, in my conscience, la! 150

King. Then keep thy vow, sirrah, when thou meet'st the fellow.

Will. So I will, my liege, as I live.

King. Who serv'st thou under?

Will. Under Captain Gower, my liege. 155

Flu. Gower is a good captain and is good knowledge and lit-
eratured in the wars.

King. Call him hither to me, soldier.

Will. I will, my liege.   *Exit.*

King. Here, Fluellen; wear thou this favour for me and stick
it in thy cap. When Alençon and myself were down together,
I pluck'd this glove from his helm. If any man challenge this,
he is a friend to Alençon and an enemy to our person. If thou
encounter any such, apprehend him, an thou dost me love. 166

Flu. Your Grace doo's me as great honours as can be desir'd
in the hearts of his subjects. I would fain see the man, that has
but two legs, that shall find himself aggrief'd at this glove, that
is all. But I would fain see it once, an please God of his grace
that I might see.   172

King. Know'st thou Gower?

Flu. He is my dear friend, an please you.

King. Pray thee go seek him and bring him to my tent. 176

Flu. I will fetch him.   *Exit.*

King. My Lord of Warwick, and my brother Gloucester,
Follow Fluellen closely at the heels.
The glove which I have given him for a favour   180
May haply purchase him a box o' th' ear;
It is the soldier's. I by bargain should
Wear it myself. Follow, good cousin Warwick.
If that the soldier strike him—as I judge
By his blunt bearing, he will keep his word—   185
Some sudden mischief may arise of it;
For I do know Fluellen valiant,
And, touch'd with choler, hot as gunpowder,
And quickly will return an injury.
Follow, and see there be no harm between them.   190
Go you with me, uncle of Exeter.   *Exeunt.*

[Scene VIII. *Before* King Henry's *pavilion.*]

Enter *Gower* and *Williams*.

Will. I warrant it is to knight you, Captain.

Enter *Fluellen*.

Flu. God's will and his pleasure, Captain, I beseech you now, come apace to the King. There is more good toward you peradventure than is in your knowledge to dream of.   5

Will. Sir, know you this glove?

Flu. Know the glove? I know the glove is a glove.

Will. I know this; and thus I challenge it.   *Strikes him.*

Flu. 'Sblood! an arrant traitor as any 's in the universal world, or in France, or in England!

Gow. How now, sir? You villain!

Will. Do you think I'll be forsworn?

Flu. Stand away, Captain Gower. I will give treason his payment into plows, I warrant you.   15

Will. I am no traitor.

Flu. That's a lie in thy throat. I charge you in his Majesty's name apprehend him. He's a friend of the Duke Alençon's.

Enter *Warwick* and *Gloucester*.

War. How now, how now? What's the matter?   20

Flu. My Lord of Warwick, here is (praised be God for it!) a most contagious treason come to light, look you, as you shall desire in a summer's day. Here is his Majesty.

Enter *King* and *Exeter*.

King. How now? What's the matter?   25

Flu. My liege, here is a villain and a traitor that, look your Grace, has struck the glove which your Majesty is take out of the helmet of Alençon.

Will. My liege, this was my glove, here is the fellow of it;
and he that I gave it to in change promis'd to wear it in his cap.
I promis'd to strike him if he did. I met this man with my
glove in his cap, and I have been as good as my word.   34

Flu. Your Majesty hear now, saving your Majesty's manhood, what an arrant, rascally, beggarly, lousy knave it is! I
hope your Majesty is pear me testimony and witness, and will
avouchment, that this is the glove of Alençon that your Majesty
is give me, in your conscience, now.   40

King. Give me thy glove, soldier. Look, here is the fellow
of it.
'Twas I indeed thou promised'st to strike;
And thou hast given me most bitter terms.   44

Flu. An please your Majesty, let his neck answer for it, if
there is any martial law in the world.

King. How canst thou make me satisfaction?

Will. All offences, my lord, come from the heart. Never
came any from mine that might offend your Majesty.   51

King. It was ourself thou didst abuse.

Will. Your Majesty came not like yourself. You appear'd
to me but as a common man; witness the night, your garments,
your lowliness. And what your Highness suffer'd under that
shape, I beseech you take it for your own fault, and not mine;
for had you been as I took you for, I made no offence. Therefore I beseech your Highness pardon me.   60

King. Here, uncle Exeter, fill this glove with crowns
And give it to this fellow. Keep it, fellow,
And wear it for an honour in thy cap
Till I do challenge it. Give him the crowns;
And, Captain, you must needs be friends with him.   65

Flu. By this day and this light, the fellow has mettle enough
in his belly. Hold, there is twelve pence for you; and I pray
you to serve God, and keep you out of prawls, and prabbles, and

quarrels, and dissensions, and, I warrant you it is the better
for you.   71

Will. I will none of your money.

Flu. It is with a good will. I can tell you it will serve you to
mend your shoes. Come, wherefore should you be so pashful?
Your shoes is not so good. 'Tis a good silling, I warrant you, or
I will change it.   77

Enter [an English] *Herald.*

King. Now, herald, are the dead numb'red?

Her. Here is the number of the slaught'red French.

[*Gives a paper.*]

King. What prisoners of good sort are taken, uncle?   80

Exe. Charles Duke of Orleans, nephew to the King;
John Duke of Bourbon and Lord Bouciqualt:
Of other lords and barons, knights and squires,
Full fifteen hundred, besides common men.

King. This note doth tell me of ten thousand French   85
That in the field lie slain. Of princes, in this number,
And nobles bearing banners, there lie dead
One hundred twenty-six; added to these,
Of knights, esquires, and gallant gentlemen,
Eight thousand and four hundred; of the which,   90
Five hundred were but yesterday dubb'd knights;
So that in these ten thousand they have lost
There are but sixteen hundred mercenaries;
The rest are princes, barons, lords, knights, squires,
And gentlemen of blood and quality.   95
The names of those their nobles that lie dead:
Charles Delabreth, High Constable of France;
Jaques of Chatillon, Admiral of France;
The master of the crossbows, Lord Rambures;
Great Master of France, the brave Sir Guichard Dauphin;   100
John Duke of Alençon; Anthony Duke of Brabant,

The brother to the Duke of Burgundy;
And Edward Duke of Bar; of lusty earls,
Grandpré and Roussi, Fauconberg and Foix,
Beaumont and Marle, Vaudemont and Lestrale.   105
Here was a royal fellowship of death!
Where is the number of our English dead?
                              [*Herald gives another paper.*]
Edward the Duke of York, the Earl of Suffolk,
Sir Richard Ketly, Davy Gam, Esquire;
None else of name; and of all other men   110
But five-and-twenty. O God, thy arm was here!
And not to us, but to thy arm alone,
Ascribe we all! When, without stratagem,
But in plain shock and even play of battle,
Was ever known so great and little loss   115
On one part and on th' other? Take it, God,
For it is only thine!
    Exe.   'Tis wonderful!
    King. Come, go we in procession to the village;
And be it death proclaimed through our host
To boast of this, or take that praise from God   120
Which is his only.
    Flu. Is it not lawful, an please your Majesty, to tell how many
is kill'd?
    King. Yes, Captain; but with this acknowledgment,
That God fought for us.   125
    Flu. Yes, my conscience, he did us great good.
    King. Do we all holy rites.
Let there be sung 'Non nobis' and 'Te Deum,'
The dead with charity enclos'd in clay,
And then to Calais; and to England then;   130
Where ne'er from France arriv'd more happy men.
                                          Exeunt.

Act V.

Enter *Chorus*.

Vouchsafe to those that have not read the story
That I may prompt them; and of such as have,
I humbly pray them to admit th' excuse
Of time, of numbers, and due course of things
Which cannot in their huge and proper life   5
Be here presented. Now we bear the King
Toward Calais. Grant him there. There seen,
Heave him away upon your winged thoughts
Athwart the sea. Behold, the English beach
Pales in the flood with men, with wives and boys,   10
Whose shouts and claps outvoice the deep-mouth'd sea,
Which, like a mighty whiffler fore the King,
Seems to prepare his way. So let him land,
And solemnly see him set on to London.
So swift a pace hath thought that even now   15
You may imagine him upon Blackheath;
Where that his lords desire him to have borne
His bruised helmet and his bended sword
Before him through the city. He forbids it,
Being free from vainness and self-glorious pride;   20
Giving full trophy, signal, and ostent
Quite from himself to God. But now behold,
In the quick forge and working house of thought,
How London doth pour out her citizens!
The Mayor and all his brethren in best sort—   25
Like to the senators of th' antique Rome,
With the plebeians swarming at their heels—
Go forth and fetch their conqu'ring Cæsar in;
As, by a lower but loving likelihood,
Were now the general of our gracious Empress   30

(As in good time he may) from Ireland coming,
Bringing rebellion broached on his sword,
How many would the peaceful city quit
To welcome him! Much more, and much more cause,
Did they this Harry. Now in London place him;   35
As yet the lamentation of the French
Invites the King of England's stay at home;
The Emperor's coming in behalf of France
To order peace between them; and omit
All the occurrences, whatever chanc'd,   40
Till Harry's back-return again to France.
There must we bring him; and myself have play'd
The interim, by rememb'ring you 'tis past.
Then brook abridgment; and your eyes advance,
After your thoughts, straight back again to France.   *Exit.*   45

[Scene I. *France. The English camp.*]

Enter *Fluellen* and *Gower.*

Gow. Nay, that's right. But why wear you your leek to-day?
Saint Davy's day is past.

Flu. There is occasions and causes why and wherefore in all
things. I will tell you ass my friend, Captain Gower. The
rascally, scauld, beggarly, lousy, pragging knave, Pistol—which
you and yourself and all the world know to be no petter than a
fellow, look you now, of no merits—he is come to me and prings
me pread and salt yesterday, look you, and bid me eat my leek.
It was in a place where I could not breed no contention with
him; but I will be so bold as to wear it in my cap till I see him
once again, and then I will tell him a little piece of my desires.

Enter *Pistol.*

Gow. Why, here he comes, swelling like a turkey cock. 15

Flu. 'Tis no matter for his swellings nor his turkey cocks. God pless you, Aunchient Pistol! you scurvy, lousy knave, God pless you!

Pist. Ha! art thou bedlam? Dost thou thirst, base Troyan, To have me fold up Parca's fatal web? 21 Hence! I am qualmish at the smell of leek.

Flu. I peseech you heartily, scurvy, lousy knave, at my desires, and my requests, and my petitions, to eat, look you, this leek. Because, look you, you do not love it, nor your affections and your appetites and your disgestions doo's not agree with it, I would desire you to eat it. |

Pist. Not for Cadwallader and all his goats.

Flu. There is one goat for you. (*Strikes him.*) Will you be so good, scauld knave, as eat it?

Pist. Base Troyan, thou shalt die! 32

Flu. You say very true, scauld knave, when God's will is. I will desire you to live in the meantime, and eat your victuals. Come, there is sauce for it. [*Strikes him.*] You call'd me yesterday mountain-squire; but I will make you to-day a squire of low degree. I pray you fall to. If you can mock a leek, you can eat a leek. 39

Gow. Enough, Captain. You have astonish'd him.

Flu. I say I will make him eat some part of my leek, or I will peat his pate four days.—Bite, I pray you. It is good for your green wound and your ploody coxcomb. 45

Pist. Must I bite?

Flu. Yes, certainly, and out of doubt, and out of question too, and ambiguities.

Pist. By this leek, I will most horribly revenge! I eat, and yet, I swear— 50

Flu. Eat, I pray you. Will you have some more sauce to your leek? There is not enough leek to swear by.

Pist. Quiet thy cudgel. Thou dost see I eat.

Flu. Much good do you, scauld knave, heartily. Nay, pray you throw none away. The skin is good for your broken coxcomb. When you take occasions to see leeks hereafter, I pray you mock at 'em; that is all.

Pist. Good.   60

Flu. Ay, leeks is good. Hold you, there is a groat to heal your pate.

Pist. Me a groat?

Flu. Yes, verily and in truth, you shall take it; or I have another leek in my pocket, which you shall eat.   66

Pist. I take thy groat in earnest of revenge.

Flu. If I owe you anything, I will pay you in cudgels. You shall be a woodmonger and buy nothing of me but cudgels. God b' wi' you, and keep you, and heal your pate.   *Exit.*

Pist. All hell shall stir for this!   72

Gow. Go, go. You are a counterfeit cowardly knave. Will you mock at an ancient tradition, begun upon an honourable respect and worn as a memorable trophy of predeceased valour, and dare not avouch in your deeds any of your words? I have seen you gleeking and galling at this gentleman twice or thrice. You thought, because he could not speak English in the native garb, he could not therefore handle an English cudgel. You find it otherwise; and henceforth let a Welsh correction teach you a good English condition. Fare ye well.   *Exit.*

Pist. Doth Fortune play the huswife with me now?   85
News have I, that my Nell is dead i' th' spital
Of malady of France;
And there my rendezvous is quite cut off.
Old I do wax, and from my weary limbs   89
Honour is cudgell'd. Well, bawd will I turn,

And something lean to cutpurse of quick hand.
To England will I steal, and there I'll steal;
And patches will I get unto these cudgell'd scars
And swear I got them in the Gallia wars.   *Exit.*

[Scene II. *France. The* French King's *Palace.*]

Enter, at one door, *King Henry, Exeter, Bedford,* [*Gloucester,*]
Warwick, [*Westmoreland,*] and other *Lords*; at another, *Queen
Isabel,* the [*French*] *King,* the *Duke of Burgundy,* [the *Princess
Katherine, Alice,*] and other *French.*

King H. Peace to this meeting, wherefore we are met!
Unto our brother France and to our sister
Health and fair time of day. Joy and good wishes
To our most fair and princely cousin Katherine.
And as a branch and member of this royalty,   5
By whom this great assembly is contriv'd,
We do salute you, Duke of Burgundy.
And, princes French, and peers, health to you all!
    France. Right joyous are we to behold your face,
Most worthy brother England. Fairly met.   10
So are you, princes English, every one.
    Queen. So happy be the issue, brother England,
Of this good day and of this gracious meeting
As we are now glad to behold your eyes—
Your eyes which hitherto have borne in them,   15
Against the French that met them in their bent,
The fatal balls of murthering basilisks.
The venom of such looks, we fairly hope,
Have lost their quality, and that this day
Shall change all griefs and quarrels into love.   20
    King H. To cry amen to that, thus we appear.

Queen. You English princes all, I do salute you.
Burg. My duty to you both, on equal love,
Great Kings of France and England! That I have labour'd
With all my wits, my pains, and strong endeavours   25
To bring your most imperial Majesties
Unto this bar and royal interview,
Your mightiness on both parts best can witness.
Since, then, my office hath so far prevail'd
That, face to face and royal eye to eye,   30
You have congreeted, let it not disgrace me
If I demand, before this royal view,
What rub or what impediment there is
Why that the naked, poor, and mangled Peace,
Dear nurse of arts, plenty, and joyful births,   35
Should not, in this best garden of the world,
Our fertile France, put up her lovely visage.
Alas, she hath from France too long been chas'd!
And all her husbandry doth lie on heaps,
Corrupting in it own fertility.   40
Her vine, the merry cheerer of the heart,
Unpruned dies; her hedges even-pleach'd,
Like prisoners wildly overgrown with hair,
Put forth disorder'd twigs; her fallow leas
The darnel, hemlock, and rank fumitory   45
Doth root upon, while that the coulter rusts
That should deracinate such savagery.
The even mead, that erst brought sweetly forth
The freckled cowslip, burnet, and green clover,
Wanting the scythe, all uncorrected, rank,   50
Conceives by idleness and nothing teems
But hateful docks, rough thistles, kecksies, burrs,
Losing both beauty and utility.
And as our vineyards, fallows, meads, and hedges,

Defective in their natures, grow to wildness,   55
Even so our houses and ourselves and children
Have lost, or do not learn for want of time,
The sciences that should become our country;
But grow like savages—as soldiers will,
That nothing do but meditate on blood—   60
To swearing and stern looks, defus'd attire,
And everything that seems unnatural.
Which to reduce into our former favour
You are assembled; and my speech entreats
That I may know the let why gentle Peace   65
Should not expel these inconveniences
And bless us with her former qualities.

    King H. If, Duke of Burgundy, you would the peace
Whose want gives growth to th' imperfections
Which you have cited, you must buy that peace   70
With full accord to all our just demands;
Whose tenures and particular effects
You have, enschedul'd briefly, in your hands.

    Burg. The King hath heard them; to the which as yet
There is no answer made.

    King H.   Well then, the peace,   75
Which you before so urg'd, lies in his answer.

    France. I have but with a cursorary eye
O'erglanc'd the articles. Pleaseth your Grace
To appoint some of your Council presently
To sit with us once more, with better heed   80
To resurvey them, we will suddenly
Pass our accept and peremptory answer.

    King H. Brother, we shall. Go, uncle Exeter,
And brother Clarence, and you, brother Gloucester,
Warwick, and Huntingdon—go with the King;   85
And take with you free power to ratify,

Augment, or alter, as your wisdoms best
Shall see advantageable for our dignity,
Anything in or out of our demands;
And we'll consign thereto. Will you, fair sister,   90
Go with the princes or stay here with us?

Queen. Our gracious brother, I will go with them.
Happily a woman's voice may do some good
When articles too nicely urg'd be stood on.

King H. Yet leave our cousin Katherine here with us.   95
She is our capital demand, compris'd
Within the fore-rank of our articles.

Queen. She hath good leave.

*Exeunt. Manent King Henry, Katherine, and the Gentle-
woman [Alice].*

King H.   Fair Katherine, and most fair!
Will you vouchsafe to teach a soldier terms
Such as will enter at a lady's ear   100
And plead his love suit to her gentle heart?

Kath. Your Majesty shall mock at me. I cannot speak your
England.

King H. O fair Katherine, if you will love me soundly with
your French heart, I will be glad to hear you confess it brokenly
with your English tongue. Do you like me, Kate?   107

Kath. Pardonnez-moi, I cannot tell vat is 'like me.'

King H. An angel is like you, Kate, and you are like an angel.

Kath. Que dit-il? Que je suis semblable à les anges?

Alice. Oui, vraiment, sauf vostre grâce, ainsi dit-il.

King. H. I said so, dear Katherine, and I must not blush to
affirm it.   117

Kath. O bon Dieu! les langues des hommes sont pleines de
tromperies.

King H. What says she, fair one? that the tongues of men are
full of deceits?   121

Alice. Oui, dat de tongues of de mans is be full of deceits. Dat is de Princesse.

King H. The Princess is the better Englishwoman. I' faith, Kate, my wooing is fit for thy understanding. I am glad thou canst speak no better English; for if thou couldst, thou wouldst find me such a plain king that thou wouldst think I had sold my farm to buy my crown. I know no ways to mince it in love but directly to say 'I love you.' Then, if you urge me farther than to say, 'Do you in faith?' I wear out my suit. Give me your answer; i' faith, do! and so clap hands and a bargain. How say you, lady?

Kath. Sauf vostre honneur, me understand well.   136

King H. Marry, if you would put me to verses or to dance for your sake, Kate, why, you undid me. For the one I have neither words nor measure; and for the other I have no strength in measure, yet a reasonable measure in strength. If I could win a lady at leapfrog, or by vaulting into my saddle with my armour on my back, under the correction of bragging be it spoken, I should quickly leap into a wife. Or if I might buffet for my love, or bound my horse for her favours, I could lay on like a butcher and sit like a jackanapes, never off. But, before God, Kate, I cannot look greenly nor gasp out my eloquence, nor I have no cunning in protestation; only downright oaths, which I never use till urg'd, nor never break for urging. If thou canst love a fellow of this temper, Kate, whose face is not worth sunburning, that never looks in his glass for love of anything he sees there, let thine eye be thy cook. I speak to thee plain soldier. If thou canst love me for this, take me; if not, to say to thee that I shall die, is true—but for thy love, by the Lord, no; yet I love thee too. And while thou liv'st, dear Kate, take a fellow of plain and uncoined constancy; for he perforce must do thee right, because he hath not the gift to woo in other places. For these fellows of infinite tongue that can rhyme themselves

into ladies' favours, they do always reason themselves out again.
What! A speaker is but a prater; a rhyme is but a ballad. A
good leg will fall, a straight back will stoop, a black beard will
turn white, a curl'd pate will grow bald, a fair face will wither,
a full eye will wax hollow; but a good heart, Kate, is the sun
and the moon; or rather, the sun, and not the moon, for it
shines bright and never changes, but keeps his course truly. If
thou would have such a one, take me; and take me, take a
soldier; take a soldier, take a king. And what say'st thou then
to my love? Speak, my fair—and fairly, I pray thee.

Kath. Is it possible dat I sould love de ennemie of France? 179

King H. No, it is not possible you should love the enemy of
France, Kate; but in loving me you should love the friend of
France; for I love France so well that I will not part with a
village of it—I will have it all mine. And, Kate, when France
is mine and I am yours, then yours is France and you are mine. 186

Kath. I cannot tell vat is dat.

King H. No, Kate? I will tell thee in French; which I am
sure will hang upon my tongue like a new-married wife about
her husband's neck, hardly to be shook off. Quand j'ai la possession de France, et quand vous avez la possession de moi (Let
me see, what then? Saint Denis be my speed!), donc vostre est
France et vous estes mienne. It is as easy for me, Kate, to
conquer the kingdom as to speak so much more French. I shall
never move thee in French, unless it be to laugh at me.   198

Kath. Sauf vostre honneur, le François que vous parlez, il
est meilleur que l'Anglois lequel je parle.

King H. No, faith, is't not, Kate. But thy speaking of my
tongue, and I thine, most truly-falsely, must needs be granted
to be much at one. But, Kate, dost thou understand thus
much English? Canst thou love me?   206

Kath. I cannot tell.

King H. Can any of your neighbours tell, Kate? I'll ask

them. Come, I know thou lovest me; and at night when you come into your closet, you'll question this gentlewoman about me; and I know, Kate, you will to her dispraise those parts in me that you love with your heart; but, good Kate, mock me mercifully; the rather, gentle Princess, because I love thee cruelly. If ever thou beest mine, Kate—as I have a saving faith within me tells me thou shalt—I get thee with scambling, and thou must therefore needs prove a good soldier-breeder. Shall not thou and I, between Saint Denis and Saint George, compound a boy, half French, half English, that shall go to Constantinople and take the Turk by the beard? Shall we not? What say'st thou, my fair flower-de-luce?

Kath. I do not know dat.   225

King H. No; 'tis hereafter to know, but now to promise. Do but now promise, Kate, you will endeavour for your French part of such a boy; and for my English moiety take the word of a king and a bachelor. How answer you, la plus belle Katherine du monde, mon très-cher et devin déesse?   232

Kath. Your Majestee ave fausse French enough to deceive de most sage damoisell dat is en France.   235

King H. Now, fie upon my false French! By mine honour in true English, I love thee, Kate; by which honour I dare not swear thou lovest me; yet my blood begins to flatter me that thou dost, notwithstanding the poor and untempering effect of my visage. Now beshrew my father's ambition! He was thinking of civil wars when he got me; therefore was I created with a stubborn outside, with an aspect of iron, that, when I come to woo ladies, I fright them. But in faith, Kate, the elder I wax, the better I shall appear. My comfort is, that old age, that ill layer-up of beauty, can do no more spoil upon my face. Thou hast me, if thou hast me, at the worst; and thou shalt wear me, if thou wear me, better and better; and therefore tell me, most fair Katherine, will you have me? Put off your

maiden blushes; avouch the thoughts of your heart with the
looks of an empress; take me by the hand, and say 'Harry of
England, I am thine!' which word thou shalt no sooner bless
mine ear withal but I will tell thee aloud 'England is thine,
Ireland is thine, France is thine, and Henry Plantagenet is
thine'; who, though I speak it before his face, if he be not fellow with the best king, thou shalt find the best king of good fellows. Come, your answer in broken music! for thy voice is music and thy English broken; therefore, queen of all Katherines,
break thy mind to me in broken English. Wilt thou have me?

Kath. Dat is as it sall please de roi mon père.

King H. Nay, it will please him well, Kate. It shall please
him, Kate.

Kath. Den it sall also content me.   270

King H. Upon that I kiss your hand and I call you my queen.

Kath. Laissez, mon seigneur, laissez, laissez! Ma foi, je ne
veux point que vous abaissiez vostre grandeur en baisant la
main d'une de vostre Seigneurie indigne serviteur. Excusez-
moi, je vous supplie, mon très-puissant seigneur.

King H. Then I will kiss your lips, Kate.

Kath. Les dames et demoiselles pour estre baisées devant leur
noces, il n'est pas la coutume de France.   281

King H. Madam my interpreter, what says she?

Alice. Dat it is not be de fashon pour de ladies of France—
I cannot tell vat is 'baiser' en Anglish.   286

King H. To kiss.

Alice. Your Majestee entendre bettre que moi.

King H. It is not a fashion for the maids in France to kiss
before they are married, would she say?   291

Alice. Oui, vraiment.

King H. O Kate, nice customs cursy to great kings. Dear
Kate, you and I cannot be confin'd within the weak list of a
country's fashion. We are the makers of manners, Kate; and

the liberty that follows our places stops the mouth of all find-faults, as I will do yours for upholding the nice fashion of your country in denying me a kiss. Therefore patiently, and yielding. [*Kisses her.*] You have witchcraft in your lips, Kate. There is more eloquence in a sugar touch of them than in the tongues of the French Council, and they should sooner persuade Harry of England than a general petition of monarchs. Here comes your father.   306

Enter the *French Power* and the *English Lords.*

Burg. God save your Majesty! My royal cousin,
Teach you our princess English?

King H. I would have her learn, my fair cousin, how perfectly I love her, and that is good English.   311

Burg. Is she not apt?

King H. Our tongue is rough, coz, and my condition is not smooth; so that, having neither the voice nor the heart of flattery about me, I cannot so conjure up the spirit of love in her that he will appear in his true likeness.   317

Burg. Pardon the frankness of my mirth if I answer you for that. If you would conjure in her, you must make a circle; if conjure up love in her in his true likeness, he must appear naked and blind. Can you blame her then, being a maid yet ros'd over with the virgin crimson of modesty, if she deny the appearance of a naked blind boy in her naked seeing self? It were, my lord, a hard condition for a maid to consign to.

King H. Yet they do wink and yield, as love is blind and enforces.

Burg. They are then excus'd, my lord, when they see not what they do.   330

King H. Then, good my lord, teach your cousin to consent winking.

Burg. I will wink on her to consent, my lord, if you will

teach her to know my meaning; for maids well summer'd and
warm kept are like flies at Bartholomew-tide, blind, though
they have their eyes; and then they will endure handling which
before would not abide looking on.   338

King H. This moral ties me over to time and a hot summer;
and so I shall catch the fly, your cousin, in the latter end, and
she must be blind too.

Burg. As love is, my lord, before it loves.

King H. It is so; and you may, some of you, thank love for
my blindness, who cannot see many a fair French city for one
fair French maid that stands in my way.   346

France. Yes, my lord, you see them perspectively—the cities
turn'd into a maid; for they are all girdled with maiden walls
that war hath never ent'red.   350

King H. Shall Kate be my wife?

France. So please you.

King H. I am content, so the maiden cities you talk of may
wait on her. So the maid that stood in the way for my wish
shall show me the way to my will.   356

France. We have consented to all terms of reason.

King H. Is't so, my lords of England?

West. The King hath granted every article:
His daughter first; and in sequel, all,   361
According to their firm proposed natures.

Exe. Only he hath not yet subscribed this: Where your
Majesty demands that the King of France, having any occasion
to write for matter of grant, shall name your Highness in this
form and with this addition, in French, 'Nostre très-cher fils
Henri, Roi d'Angleterre, héritier de France'; and thus in
Latin, 'Praecarissimus filius noster Henricus, Rex Angliae et
haeres Franciae.'   370

France. Nor this I have not, brother, so denied
But your request shall make me let it pass.

King H. I pray you then, in love and dear alliance,
Let that one article rank with the rest,
And thereupon give me your daughter. 375
France. Take her, fair son, and from her blood raise up
Issue to me, that the contending kingdoms
Of France and England, whose very shores look pale
With envy of each other's happiness,
May cease their hatred; and this dear conjunction 380
Plant neighbourhood and Christianlike accord
In their sweet bosoms, that never war advance
His bleeding sword 'twixt England and fair France.
Lords. Amen!
King H. Now, welcome, Kate; and bear me witness all 385
That here I kiss her as my sovereign queen.

Flourish.

Queen. God, the best maker of all marriages,
Combine your hearts in one, your realms in one!
As man and wife, being two, are one in love,
So be there 'twixt your kingdoms such a spousal 390
That never may ill office, or fell jealousy,
Which troubles oft the bed of blessed marriage,
Thrust in between the paction of these kingdoms
To make divorce of their incorporate league;
That English may as French, French Englishmen, 395
Receive each other! God speak this Amen!
All. Amen!
King H. Prepare we for our marriage; on which day,
My Lord of Burgundy, we'll take your oath,
And all the peers', for surety of our leagues. 400
Then shall I swear to Kate, and you to me,
And may our oaths well kept and prosp'rous be!

Sennet. Exeunt.

[EPILOGUE.]

Enter *Chorus.*

Thus far, with rough and all-unable pen,
  Our bending author hath pursu'd the story,
In little room confining mighty men,
  Mangling by starts the full course of their glory.
Small time; but in that small, most greatly lived   5
  This Star of England. Fortune made his sword;
By which the world's best garden he achieved,
  And of it left his son imperial lord.
Henry the Sixth, in infant bands crown'd King
  Of France and England, did this king succeed;   10
Whose state so many had the managing
  That they lost France and made his England bleed;
Which oft our stage hath shown; and for their sake
In your fair minds let this acceptance take.   [*Exit.*]

NOTES

Cf. use of Chorus in Heywood's *Edward IV* (Shakespeare Society ed., p. 124); Greene's *Alphonsus*; and *The Play of Stucley*.

8. gentles: gentlemen and ladies.

9. flat unraised spirits: uninspired intellects.

10. scaffold. The Elizabethan stage structure was unsubstantial, compared with that of the modern theatre, and it projected into the auditorium (pit, or orchestra). Hence it might well be called a *scaffold*. The word also suggests the temporary platforms in the inn yards on which plays were presented before the first English theatre was built and which some of the audience could still remember.—**Cockpit.** The theatre was circular or octagonal, and the seats rose in tiers, so that it was not unlike the pits in which cockfights were held.

13. O: circle.—**the very casques.** The theatre would be too small to hold 'even the helmets' worn at Agincourt.

16. Attest: stand for.—**in little place:** not taking up much room.

17. us: i.e., us actors, for whom the Prologue speaks.—**to:** in comparison with.—**this great accompt:** this great amount, or sum (i.e., the great subject which the actors are to set forth).

18. your imaginary forces: the powers of your imagination.

25. puissance: forces, troops. The word is sometimes trisyllabic (as here), sometimes dissyllabic.

28. deck. I.e., with appropriate splendour of costume.

30. th' accomplishment of many years: the deeds done in many years.

31. for the which supply: to fill up the defects just mentioned (i.e., by describing what the players cannot act or represent).

33. Prologue-like: in the guise of a Prologue, or in the manner of a Prologue—probably the former, the Prologue having a conventional costume.

The gist of the whole Chorus is, then, an apology, with an appeal to the audience to use their imagination and a promise to explain or fill in what the action cannot afford. The other choruses are to much the same effect.

Act I. Scene I.

The effect of the first act is to relieve King Henry, in the minds of the audience, of any responsibility for the war that is to ensue. The clergy take it all upon their consciences. We also have the most favourable exposition of the justice of his cause. And at the end of the act the Dauphin's wanton insult adds the touch of personal injury which makes the conflict interesting as the King's own war rather than as a mere matter of political aggrandizement.

1. self: selfsame.—**urg'd:** proposed, mentioned,—not necessarily 'pressed.'

3. Was like, etc.: was likely (to pass), and would in fact have passed.

4. scambling: scrambling, turbulent. Cf. Lyly, *Sapho and Phao*, iii, 2: 'I am in the depth of my learning driven to a muse, how this Lent I shall scamble in the court' (Fairholt ed., I, 185); *ibid.*, iv, 3: 'scambling to catch hold to harbor in the house he had made, he [the stockdove] fell from the bough' (I, 201); Drayton, *Muses Elizium*, 74: '*Scatter Nuts, and for them scamble*' (Spenser Society ed., 82).

9. temporal lands: estates not actually used for worship or devotion.

15. lazars: lepers—but used rather loosely for those afflicted with other similar diseases as well.—**age:** aged persons (abstract for concrete).

21. **what prevention?** What can we do to forestall such action?

22. **fair regard:** kindly consideration.

24. **The courses of his youth.** King Henry's riotous youth had been set before the Elizabethan playgoers in the First and Second Parts of Shakespeare's *Henry IV*.

26. **mortified:** killed, or brought to death's door.

29. **th' offending Adam:** original sin, the hereditary sinfulness inherited from Adam. Also called 'the old Adam,' from the biblical phrase.

34. **heady currance:** impetuous current.

36. **all at once:** everything (i.e., all its power over him) at the same time.

38. **divinity:** theology.

43–44. **List . . . music.** Cf. *Edward III*, ii, 1 (*Shakespeare Apocrypha*, ed. Brooke, 74).

45. **policy:** statecraft, diplomacy.

47. **that:** so that.

48. **charter'd:** privileged.—**libertine.** Used of all kinds of unrestraint, not exclusively in the limited modern sense. Cf. 'The wind bloweth where it listeth.'

49. **the mute wonder lurketh in men's ears:** wonder keeps men silent and makes them listen eagerly.

51–52. **the art and practic part of life,** etc.: since the King never studied any of these subjects, he must have acquired his knowledge of their 'theory' from experience in practical life.[1]

---

[1] Cf. Heywood, *The English Traveller*, i, 1: 'Oh friend, that I to mine owne Notion Had ioyned but your experience; I haue the Theoricke, But you the Practicke' (Pearson ed., IV, 7); Dekker, *Worke for Armourers*: 'Your Commanders had too much of the *Martiall Theoricke*, your souldiers too little of the *Practicke*' (*Non-Dramatic Works*, ed. Grosart, IV, 92).

Yet that does not decrease the wonder of it all, since his pursuits were not such as to give him experience in such matters.

These speeches prepare us for the great change which we are to see in Henry since he became King.

53. **glean it:** pick it up by the way.

54. **vain:** idle, empty-headed.

55. **rude:** uncultivated.

58. **sequestration:** separation.

59. **popularity:** association with the common people—almost, low company.

61. **wholesome berries,** etc. This was a common theory in gardening.

64. **which:** i.e., his contemplation, and the wisdom that resulted from it.

66. **crescive in his faculty:** increasing in its strength.

68. **means.** Emphatic.

70. **bill.** Emphatic. Ely calls Canterbury to the real subject of discussion.

71. **Urg'd.** See note on l. 1.

72. **indifferent:** impartial.

73. **upon our part:** towards our side.

74. **cherishing th' exhibiters against us:** favouring those who make representations, or proposals, against us.

76. **Upon:** as the result of.—**spiritual Convocation:** the assembly of the spiritual, or religious, dignitaries.

77. **in regard of:** in consideration of.

78. **open'd:** expounded, explained.

81. **part withal:** part with. *Withal* is often so used at the end of a clause.

86. **severals:** details.—**unhidden passages:** well-known facts.

Scene II.

The dignity and seriousness of King Henry, for which the preceding scene has prepared us, are emphasized the moment he begins to speak. The occasion lends itself readily to this, and the royal *we* is used with much consistency.

3. **liege:** liege lord.

4. **be resolv'd:** have our doubts cleared up.

6. **task:** occupy, trouble.

9. **proceed:** i.e., taking up the explanation where it was interrupted in our previous talk (see i, 1, 90 ff.).

11. **Law Salique:** the so-called Salic Law, which settled the crown of France on heirs male only.

12. **or . . . or:** either . . . or.

14. **your reading:** your interpretation of the law.

15. **nicely charge your understanding soul:** be so foolish as to burden your soul (which understands the truth of the matter) with guilt. The antithesis between *nicely* and *understanding* is quite in the formal and balanced style appropriate to the serious speeches of the historical drama.

16. **opening:** setting forth.—**miscreate:** miscreated, unrighteously fabricated.

17. **in native colours:** i.e., in the colours that they have by nature. Such titles would have to be *coloured* by art to make them look like the truth.

18. **God doth know:** God only knows.

19, 20. **in approbation Of:** in proving the justice of—i.e., by an appeal to the judgment of war.

27. **wrong:** wrongful acts.

29. **conjuration:** solemn adjuration.

35. **imperial:** so called as reigning over more kingdoms than one. The adjective subtly forecasts the archbishop's intention to urge the King to assert his claim to France. For a discussion of

the Salic Law, see *Egerton Papers* (Camden Society, Series 1, Vol. XII, p. 38).

37. **Pharamond:** an old king of the Salian Franks.

40. **gloze:** gloss, interpret (often with a suggestion of a forced or tricky interpretation).

42. **female bar:** prohibition to women.

49. **dishonest:** dishonourable.

59. **Idly:** foolishly, without good reason.

72. **fine:** furnish.

74. **Convey'd himself as:** fraudulently passed himself off as.

88. **Lewis his.** A form of the genitive common in the six-teenth and seventeenth centuries, and occasionally found later. It is due to a mistaken idea that the *-es* (or *'s*) of the genitive stands for the pronoun *his.*—**appear:** are clearly seen.

93. **to hide them in a net:** to resort to a transparent subter-fuge. A proverbial expression.

94. **amply to imbare:** to lay bare completely.

96. **May I,** etc. After all this argument it is proper that the King should sum the question up in this direct and simple way. It has the effect of honesty and straightforwardness and leaves the audience with no doubt of his good faith, whatever they may think of the eloquent ecclesiastics.

98. **the Book of Numbers.** Cf. *Numbers,* xxvii, 8. It was customary to seek authority for modern law and practice in special Hebrew legislation in the Old Testament.

107. **defeat:** destruction. The allusion is to the Battle of Crécy in 1346 (cf. ii, 4, 54).

111. **entertain:** receive.

114. **for action:** for want of something to do. A common old sense of *for.*

123. **rouse yourself.** Cf. Peele, *Edward I* (*Works,* ed. Bullen, I, 181): 'To rouse him lion-like'; Marlowe, *1 Tamburlaine,* i, 2,

52: 'As princely lions when they rouse themselves' (ed. Ellis-Fermor, 80).

126. **So hath your Highness.** *Hath* is the emphatic word. *Your grace* and *your highness*, as well as *your majesty*, were formerly used in addressing kings.

129. **pavilion'd:** tented, encamped.

136. **We must not,** etc. The King's conscientious scruples are satisfied. His caution, however, appears in what follows. The result of the whole method of presentation is to make the French War seem to have been entered upon, not upon any impulse of Henry's, but with the utmost deliberation. It is set forth almost as a holy war.

137. **lay down our proportions:** plan our levies of troops.

138. **road:** inroad.

139. **With all advantages:** whenever he sees a good opportunity.

140. **marches:** borders.

141. **Shall:** surely will.

144. **the main intendment of the Scot:** the purpose of the whole body of the Scottish nation.

145. **still:** always.—**giddy:** fickle, untrustworthy.

151. **Galling:** worrying. To *gall* is properly to 'excoriate,' 'knock off the skin.' It is often used figuratively by Shakespeare. —**Gleaned:** already stripped of its defenders. Cf. l. 153. Or perhaps proleptic.—**assays:** attacks, forays.

153. **That:** so that.—**defence:** defenders.

155. **fear'd:** frightened.

156. **hear her but exampled by herself:** listen to an example to Englishmen taken from the history of England itself. This refers to the captivity of David II.

160. **impounded as a stray.** Said contemptuously—'put into the pound,' as was done with cattle found wandering out of their owner's fields.

165. **sumless:** uncounted, incalculable.

166. **very old.** So old, indeed, that the final *e* of *France* is pronounced—'If that you will Francë win.' Cf. Fynes Moryson, *Itinerary*, ed. 1617, Pt. II, p. 3:

> *He that will England winne,*
> *Must with Ireland first beginne.*

169. **in prey:** absent in search of prey.

172. **Playing the mouse,** etc. The proverb alluded to is still in common use—'While the cat's away the mice will play.'

175. **a crush'd necessity:** a forced (or illogical) conclusion as to necessity. The point is that the conclusion that 'the cat must stay at home' is not the natural inference from what has been said; the natural inference is rather that which he proceeds to point to—that traps must be set for the mice. The Quartos have *curst necessity*, which many editors adopt.

177. **pretty . . . petty.** The jingle is of course intentional. It emphasizes the light tone of the speech and expresses contempt for the Scots.

179. **advised:** considerate, wise.

181. **consent:** harmony, agreement—uniting the meaning of *consent* and *concent*.

182. **Congreeing:** agreeing together—more emphatic than *agreeing* simply.—**close.** In the musical sense.

183. **True!** Supplied from Quartos by Capell.

186. **butt:** the structure of turf to which the target was fixed in archery contests. Hence, 'end and aim,' 'limit,' etc. Cf. *Othello*, v, 2, 267: 'here is my butt.'

187. **honeybees.** For the passage, cf. Lyly, *Euphues*, ed. Croll and Clemons, pp. 242–244.

189. **The act of order:** the method and operations of orderly, well-regulated society and government.

197. **busied in his majesty:** i.e., as busy in his royal office as they are in their humbler positions.

199. **civil:** well-behaved, peaceable and orderly.

200. **mechanic.** Almost always used in Elizabethan England of humble toilers, with a suggestion of contempt or pity or condescension.

202. **sad-ey'd:** serious-eyed—not 'sorrowful.'

203. **executors** (accented on the first syllable): executioners.

205–206. **having full reference To one consent:** conducing altogether to one harmonious purpose.

208. **as many ways.** Notice metre.

210. **dial's:** a sun-dial is meant, not the dial of a clock.

211. **afoot:** under way.

212. **borne:** carried out.

213. **Without defeat:** without being thwarted in their individual operations.

216. **withal:** with *that*.

217. **powers:** forces.

220. **policy:** statecraft, statesmanship.

222. **are we well resolv'd:** all our doubts and scruples are well settled.

225. **Or there:** either there.

233. **worshipp'd:** honoured.—**waxen.** Emphatic—'even with an epitaph so little durable as one engraved in wax would be.'

238. **render:** report.

242. **grace:** virtue, Christian self-control.

243. **fett'red,** etc. The passions are thought of as here under control as much as prisoners are in their cells.

245. **few:** in brief, in short. For the Dauphin's message, cf. *Edward III*, iv, 4 (*Shakespeare Apocrypha*, ed. Brooke, p. 94); and, for the tennis-ball story, see C. L. Kingsford, *English Historical Literature in the Fifteenth Century*, p. 41 (and index); J. H. Wylie, *The Reign of Henry the Fifth*, I, 405 note, 425–430; and O. Emmerig, in *Englische Studien*, XXXIX (1908), 362 ff.

248. Notice the metre.

251. **be advis'd:** consider.

252. **galliard:** a lively dance.

254. **meeter for your spirit:** as being more appropriate to your disposition.

255. **in lieu of this:** in return for this.

261. **When we have match'd,** etc. In what follows the King uses rather elaborately the technical language of court tennis.

263. **Shall:** which shall. The omission of the relative in the nominative is very common.—**The hazard:** again a technical tennis term. Cf. Webster (ed. Lucas), I, 248; *The Hog Hath Lost his Pearl*, i, 1: 'he is a gentleman whom it hath pleased fortune to make her tennis-ball of, and therefore to be struck by every fool into hazard' (Dodsley's *Old Plays*, ed. Collier, VI, 334).

266. **chases.** Another tennis term. Cf. *The Country Gentleman's Vade Mecum* (1699), p. 54: 'When he hears the Marker calling Forty, Love, and a Chace.'

267. **comes o'er us with:** twits us with, reproaches us with.

268. **what use we made of them.** The King here suggests that he had a deliberate purpose in playing the roisterer in his youth, or at all events that he has derived from his riots useful experience. This latter suggestion has already been made in the first scene by the Archbishop of Canterbury; see ll. 51 ff. We may compare also Prince Hal's speech near the beginning of *1 Henry IV*. None of these observations, however, need be taken very seriously. No one can doubt that the Prince was wild, for he enjoyed the society of Falstaff and his other companions. There is a distinct chasm between the character of Prince Hal in the two parts of *Henry IV* and the character of Henry V when he becomes king. Were the change only a moral one, it might well enough be understood, since there is nothing in *Henry IV* to indicate that the Prince's character had become corrupt; it is an intellectual change as well. The character of the

Prince's mind is keen, quick-witted, lively in every possible way. His mental processes are like flashes of lightning. The mental operations of King Henry V are solid, dignified, and deliberate. It is not too much to say that we have two entirely distinct persons. Prince Hal could never have developed into this kind of Henry V.

270. **living hence:** i.e., living out of England. The King means that his thoughts were ever in France, 'since our real residence was not in England—since, when we were in England, we were really *away from home*, France being our home.'

272. **from home:** away from home.

273. **keep my state:** maintain my royal dignity.

275. **When I do rouse me in my throne of France.** *Rouse* suggests the alert attitude of one who, while sitting, is yet ready at any moment to spring to his feet.

282. **gunstones.** Cannon balls were originally made of stone, not metal.

283. **charged:** burdened with guilt or responsibility.—**wasteful:** devastating.

289. **But this lies all,** etc. The King has shown a certain amount of excitement, but now he masters it and resumes his original solemnity of demeanour. This appeal to God would of course be impossible but for the elaborate exposition of the ecclesiastics in the preceding scene. They have made out that this war is an assertion of a sacred right, that it is indeed a kind of holy war.

297. **Convey them:** escort them.—**conduct:** guidance and protection. 300. **omit:** let slip, neglect.—**happy:** fortunate, opportune.

304. **proportions:** levies. Cf. i, 2, 137: 'Lay down our proportions to defend against the Scots.'

307. **God before:** God going before, under the guidance of God, with God's help. An old phrase, not to be confounded with

'before God.' Cf. Kyd, *Cornelia*, iii, 3 (ed. Boas, 130): 'god to fore.'

309. task his thought: tax his thought.

ACT II. Prologue.

---

2. silken dalliance: social pleasure, which has been put off with the robes of silk, appropriate to it.

9. hilts: hilt. The plural is common because each of the parts of the hilt in our sense was called a hilt.

10. crowns imperial: i.e., crowns worn by those who rule over more than one kingdom.

12. advis'd: informed.—**intelligence:** spies.

14. policy: diplomacy.

16. Model to thy inward greatness. This expression is by no means clear. Some have wished to read 'module,' i.e., a small thing, and to take *to* as meaning 'compared with' (a common sense). England would then be apostrophized as a little thing in comparison with the greatness of her minds, which would excellently fit the next line.

18. that honour would thee do: that honour would have thee do.

20. thy fault: Englishmen were regularly accused of treachery in the Middle Ages because of their frequent revolts against their kings.

26. gilt. The pun on *gilt* and *guilt* was so common in the Elizabethan time that it may almost be called an idiom. Of course it was not intended here to raise a laugh. Cf. Lady Macbeth's speech 'I'll gild the faces of the grooms withal, For it must seem their guilt' (ii, 2, 56, 57).

27. fearful: frightened.

28. **this grace of kings:** this honour of kings, this person who confers honour on the kingly station.

31, 32. **Linger your patience on:** Let your patience hold out. —**well digest Th' abuse of distance:** accept without objection the illusion as to distance which we would have you feel. To digest a thing is to assimilate it in such a fashion that it causes no distress. Hence the audience are bidden, as it were, to swallow the barefaced deception as to actual distance which the exigencies of this drama necessitate, and not to let the mouthful disagree with them. Cf. *An Abridgment of Bishop Burnet's History*, ed. Rev. Thomas Stackhouse, p. 39: 'What made his [Sir Henry Vane's] death not so well digested was an unaccountable clemency extended to some who were thought equally culpable'; Marlowe, *1 Tamburlaine*, iii, 2 (ed. Dyce, I, 55; ed. Ellis-Fermor, p. 120): 'Your offensive rape . . . Hath seem'd to be digested long ago.' The Folio reading is *wee'l* (*we'll* F₃F₄). Pope's correction (*well*) is certain.

32. **Force a play!** by the violent exercise of your imagination, fill out those acts in the play which we cannot represent.

39. **pass:** passage.—**if we may:** if we can help it. A common idiom. The literal meaning is 'if we have any power under the circumstances.' Hence, when the phrase is used with a negative in the main clause it is well rendered by our modern 'if we can help it.' Cf. *The Pedlers Prophecie*, Malone Society, l. 440: 'He shal not come in our house truly if I may.'

40. **We'll not offend one stomach,** etc.: we'll offend nobody's taste—with a pun, of course, on seasickness.

41. **till the King come forth:** i.e., when the King comes forth. The audience is bidden to imagine the scene as shifted to Southampton when that scene comes in which the King enters, namely, the beginning of scene ii.

Scene I.

1. Corporal Nym. Nym is a new character, not found in either part of *Henry IV*. His name comes from the old verb, A. S. *niman*; German, *nehman*, 'to take'; and is sufficiently appropriate to his character as a thief.[1] Bardolph and Pistol are old friends of ours from *Henry IV*.

2. Good morrow: good morning.

5. For my part, etc. Nym's style of talking is that of the person who says less than he means, indulging in awful threats of what he means to do.

6. when time shall serve, there shall be smiles: i.e., I will make up my quarrel with Pistol when the proper time comes, but not before.

7. but that shall be as it may. This implies that the time for reconciliation may never come and that Nym does not care if it doesn't.—**I dare not fight,** etc. This is said with awful irony. O yes, I am a coward, no doubt, but there is one thing I can do, I can shut my eyes (wink) and hold out my sword. Of course Nym means by this to suggest that he is really a dangerous antagonist.

9. what though: what of it. All that follows is in the same mood of awful hinting and ironical threatening.

[1] Cf. Taylor the Water Poet, *Works* (1630), Spenser Society ed., p. 71; Fairholt, *Lord Mayors' Pageants*, Percy Society, ii, 230: 'Tom Nim' (a thief); *The Puritan Widow*, i, 4 (*Shakespeare Apocrypha*, ed. Brooke, 227); Middleton, *Your Five Gallants*, i, 1 (ed. Bullen, III, 135): 'nimming away jewels and favours from gentlemen' (see also *ib.*, 149, 161, and VI, 135); Middleton and Rowley, *The Spanish Gipsy*, ii, 1 (Gayley, *Representative English Comedies*, III, 135); Gay, *Beggar's Opera*, i, 10 (Mrs. Inchbald, *British Theatre*, VI, 21): 'Nimming Ned' (see also ii, 10, *ib.*, p. 41); Hake, *Newes out of Powles Churchyard*, 1579, ed. Edmonds, sig. C. iii: 'That *Nummus* shall be nymmed streight'; Day, *The Isle of Gulls*, ed. Bullen, p. 67: 'I nimde his Chayne, and drew his Purse'; *Albumazar*, iii, 7: 'The cunning'st nimmer Of the whole company of cutpurse-hall' (Dodsley's *Old Plays*, ed. Collier, VII, 168).

13. **sworn brothers:** brethren in arms—after the old fashion of taking an oath to stand by each other and share good fortune and bad alike.

15. **I will live,** etc. Nym is still implacable. Pistol may kill him if he can, but he can't kill him until his time comes and he may happen to kill Pistol first.

17, 18. **That is my rest:** that is my determination. A phrase from Primero, an old game at cards, in which when a person was satisfied with the cards he held and was willing to rest his chances of winning upon them, he said, 'I set up my rest,' that is, 'I am determined, resolved, fixed.'

18. **that is the rendezvous of it:** that is what it all comes to, that is what it all amounts to.

19. **It is certain,** etc. We here learn for the first time the cause of the quarrel between Nym and Pistol.

20. **Nell Quickly:** that is, the hostess of the Boar's Head in Eastcheap, Falstaff's favourite tavern.

22. **I cannot tell,** etc. Nym still threatens with an affectation of saying less than he means. In what follows he suggests that he may cut Pistol's throat sometime if Pistol has it with him when he is asleep, as men occasionally do.

25, 26. **Though patience be a tired mare, yet she will plod:** Though I am almost at the end of my patience, yet it will last a little longer. Still, there must be conclusions, i.e., the end must come sometime, and then let Pistol look out for himself.

31. **tyke:** hound.

39. **if he be not drawn:** i.e., see if he hasn't drawn his sword.

42. **offer nothing here:** i.e., don't offer to fight each other here.

43. **Pish!** Nym accompanies this interjection with some scornful gesture, such as snapping his fingers in Pistol's face.

44. **Iceland dog.** There was, and is, a kind of terrier called an Iceland terrier, with sharp ears. We may imagine that Nym, in

accordance with his secretive and darkly hinting character, is represented as thin, with his hair cut short, and his ears thus appearing to stand out. Cf. Hazlitt, *Remains of the Early Popular Poetry of England*, III, 284: 'Standes lyke an Island curre'; Deloney, *Gentle Craft* (ed. Lange, 62; ed. Mann, 111): 'turning up like the tail of an Island dog'; Andrew Boorde, *Introduction and Dyetary* (ed. Furnivall), 142, 336; *Arden of Feversham*, iii, 2 (ed. Warnke, p. 36; ed. Brooke, p. 17): 'that prick-eard cur'; *Calisto and Melebea*, Malone Society, l. 1019: 'prikyeryd curr'; *The Returne from Pernassus*, ii, 5 (ed. Macray, p. 107): 'prick-eard curres'; *Ram-Alley*, iii, 1 (Dodsley's *Old Plays*, ed. Collier, V, 409).

45, 46. **show thy valour and put up your sword.** The confusion is expressed not merely by the intensity of her requests, but by their use both of the familiar *thou* and the respectful *you*. We must remember that she had been trothplight to Corporal Nym and hence was in the habit of *theeing* and *thouing* him affectionately.

47. **Will you shog off?** i.e., move away. In accordance with Pistol's suggestion that they should not fight in so public a place. Cf. Child, *English and Scottish Popular Ballads*, Pt. 6, p. 332, No. 166, st. 14: 'shogged them to Shrewsburye'; 'The Scottish Field' (ed. Robson in *Chetham Miscellanies*, Vol. II), p. 4: 'shoggeth [i.e., hastens] over the water'; Milton, *The Reason of Church Government*, in *English Prose Writings* (ed. Morley), 114.

49. **'Solus.'** Pistol does not understand *solus* and regards it as a term of abuse.

50. **mervailous:** marvellous—an old form, used by Pistol in accordance with his habit of quoting from plays and speaking in the language of tragedy. The accent is on the second syllable.

55. **take:** take offence; understand, feel, and resent an insult. —**cock is up.** Cf. *Amends for Ladies*, i, 2 (in Dodsley's *Old*

Plays, ed. Collier, XIII, 18); Dekker, *If This Be Not a Good Play* (Pearson ed., III, 309).

57. **Barbason:** a fiend.—**conjure me:** drive me away, frighten me by a threat. Pistol uses many sentences of high-sounding jargon. Nym compares Pistol's bombast to the unintelligible language of conjuration.

58, 59. **indifferently well:** tolerably well, pretty well—once more an ironical understatement.

60. **scour:** thrash. Cf. *Work for Cutlers*, p. 5 (in Hindley, *The Old Book Collector's Miscellany*, Vol. II).

61. **in fair terms:** in good style.

63. **that's the humour of it:** that's the way I feel about it, that's the state of the case. Cf. Ford and Dekker, *The Sun's Darling*, iii, 1 (ed. Weber, II, 361; ed. Dyce, III, 136).

65. **doting death.** The senseless epithet *doting* is used by Pistol merely because of its alliterating with *death*.

66. **exhale:** breathe forth thy life, die.

68. **Hilts.** See note on ii, Prologue, 9.

70. **mickle:** great. Pistol is a coward, and when Bardolph makes so vigorous a demonstration he is quite ready to shake hands with Nym.

72. **tall:** courageous.

73. **I will cut thy throat,** etc. Nym looks dark and grumbles. This threat of his explains, if explanation is necessary, the similar threat in ll. 23–25.—**in fair terms:** in good shape, in good style.

75. **Couple a gorge!** Pistol has picked up a few words of French, perhaps in preparation for his foreign campaign. What he means is *couper la gorge*, 'to cut the throat.' Nym's refusal to shake hands sets Pistol off again.

77. **O hound of Crete.** Doubtless a tag from some old play.

78. **spital:** hospital.

79. **powd'ring tub:** a tub in which beef was powdered, i.e., salted.

80. **lazar:** leper. According to Henryson's *Testament of Cressid*, Cressida was punished by the god of love for her faithlessness to Troilus by being smitten with leprosy.—**kite:** a kite was a bird of prey, of ignoble lineage, as compared with the falcon. The word is sometimes used for a faithless woman. In Chaucer's *Squire's Tale* the falcon's mate is enticed away by a kite.—**Cressid:** the heroine of Chaucer's poem, *Troilus and Criseyde*. She became a symbol for unfaithfulness in love, because she transferred her affections from Troilus to Diomede. The same story is worked up very cynically in Shakespeare's *Troilus and Cressida*. Cf. Greene, *Mamillia* (*Prose Works*, ed. Grosart, II, 16): 'There was litle cōstancy in such kites of *Cressids* kind'; New Shakspere Society, *Transactions*, 1800–1885, Pt. 2, p. 442.

83. **For the only she:** as the only woman in the world for me. *She* was used not uncommonly as a noun. Cf. *As You Like It*, iii, 1, 9, 10:

> Run, run, Orlando! carve on every tree
> The fair, the chaste, the inexpressive she.

—**pauca:** few words, enough said.

84. **Go to!** Used to dismiss the subject defiantly and contemptuously.

85. **Mine host Pistol.** The boy uses the same form of address which so offended Pistol when employed by Bardolph in l. 30.

90. **Away, you rogue!** Bardolph always resents jests at his inflamed complexion.

91, 92. **yield the crow a pudding:** a proverbial expression for 'die.' Cf. Deloney, *The Gentle Craft* (ed. Lange, Pt. 2, p. 37; ed. Mann, 163): 'Let no man triumph so much over thee to say thou gavest the crow a pudding because love would let thee live no longer.'

92, 93. **kill'd his heart.** I.e., by punishing him; 'he has broken his heart,' as we would say.

93. **presently:** instantly.

97. **Let floods o'erswell, and fiends for food howl on!** This sounds defiant. Pistol in his turn is now disinclined to accept reconciliation.

100. **Base is the slave that pays.** Cf. Heywood, *2 Fair Maid of the West* (Pearson ed., II, 416).

102. **As manhood shall compound:** i.e., we will settle this debt by fighting it out like men.

106. **'Sword' is an oath,** etc. Pistol, once more cowed by Bardolph, pretends to give way in consideration of the sacredness of the oath which Bardolph has sworn.

109. **put up:** put up your sword, sheathe your sword.

112. **A noble:** one third of a pound. Not quite the full amount of the debt, but satisfactory to Pistol because present pay—i.e., cash down—is promised.

114. **I'll live by Nym,** etc.: i.e., by means of Nym. Very likely there is a pun, whether Pistol intends it or not, since *nym* means 'to take' and Pistol expects to live by thievery.

116. **just:** correct. —**sutler.** Cf. *Fidele and Fortunio; The Two Italian Gentlemen* (Malone Society), ll. 57 ff.

121. **Well, then, that's the humour of't:** Well, then, this is how I feel about it. Nym accompanies these words by giving Pistol his hand.

124. **quotidian tertian.** In a quotidian ague the fit came every day; in a tertian ague, every other day. The hostess has mixed her terms, as usual.

127, 128. **hath run bad humours on the knight:** has forced the knight to put up with disagreeable treatment. *Humour*, it will be seen, is Nym's pet word, which he uses in all sorts of vague ways.

128. **that's the even of it:** that is exactly what it amounts to.

130. **fracted:** broken.—**corroborate:** properly 'strengthen,' but misused by Pistol to mean 'broken to pieces.'

132. **He passes some humours and careers:** He makes people put up with various whims and queer courses of action (more of Nym's peculiar dialect). Cf. Blundeville, *The Art of Riding* (1597), Bk. II, chap. 26, p. 33: 'How and when to teach your horse to passe a swift Cariere.'

133. **for, lambkins, we will live.** This seems to have no logical connection with what precedes, and probably is not intended to have any such connection.

Scene II.

1. **these traitors.** In that part of the conference which we must imagine to have preceded the entrance of Exeter and the rest, Exeter has explained the treason and mentioned the traitors. The audience is prepared to understand what he now says on account of the information given in the chorus to this act.

2. **apprehended by-and-by:** arrested very soon.

5. **Crowned.** The figure is that of allegiance as ruling in their natures.

6. **note:** knowledge.

8. **bedfellow:** bosom friend.

9. **dull'd and cloy'd.** A pair of words expressing practically the same idea, of which, however, the second is, as very commonly, more definite than the first.

10. **That he should:** to think that he should.

14. **give me your thoughts:** attend carefully to what I say.

15. **pow'rs:** forces.

18. **in head:** in an armed force.

22. **grows not in a fair consent:** does not act in perfect harmony with our sentiments.

30. **Have steep'd their galls in honey:** have changed their resentment to affection. *Gall* is frequently used for resentment

or the capacity for resentment. Cf. *Othello*, iv, 3, 95, 96:

> We have galls; and though we have some grace,
> Yet have we some revenge.

Cf. also *Hamlet*, ii, 2, 604, 605:

> I am pigeon-liver'd and lack gall
> To make oppression bitter.

31. **create of:** made of, composed of.

33. **shall forget the office of our hand:** shall forget how to use our hands. The phrase is suggested by the biblical 'If I forget thee, O Jerusalem, let my right hand forget her cunning' (*Psalms*, cxxxvii, 5).

38. **To do your Grace:** expressing result, 'so as to do.'

40. **Enlarge:** release.—**committed:** committed to prison.

43. **on his more advice:** now that he has had a chance to reflect.

44. **security:** carelessness.

46. **by his sufferance:** because he has been allowed to escape with impunity.—**more.** Emphatic.

53. **orisons:** prayers.

54. **proceeding on distemper:** resulting from physical disorder—here the physical disturbance caused by drunkenness. A man is in a temper when all the four humours are properly balanced in his constitution. Any undue disturbance of this balance results in distemper, disorder of mind or body.

55. **wink'd at:** disregarded. *To wink* formerly meant 'to close the eyes.'—**how shall we stretch our eye:** how shall we contemplate with eyes sufficiently wide open—i.e., how shall we estimate at their proper enormity.

57. **yet:** in spite of all you say.

61–63. **the late commissioners:** the persons lately appointed to act as a commission in England in place of the King while he is absent in France.—**it:** i.e., a position on the commission. It was common to use *it* with reference to a noun implied but not expressed in something that preceded.

66. **there is yours:** i.e., your commission. The King hands to each of the traitors an order of arrest on the charge of high treason.

79. **quick:** alive.

82. **your own reasons:** i.e., the reasons that they have given for the punishment of the drunken railer.

86. **apt:** ready. Much more active in sense than in modern English.—**accord:** consent.

87. **appertinents:** appurtenances.

89. **lightly:** with levity, easily, without consideration or scruple. The pun expresses contempt.

90. **practices:** plots.

96. **counsels:** secrets.

99. **Wouldst thou have practis'd on me for thy use:** i.e., if thou hadst wished to work upon my favour for thy personal advantage.

102. **finger:** emphatic, 'even my finger.'

103, 104. **stands off as gross As black and white:** is as plain as black is when contrasted with white. *Gross* meant literally 'great' and then frequently signified 'obvious,' 'palpable,' 'easily seen.' Cf. Prince Hal's pun in *1 Henry IV*, ii, 4, 249, 250: 'These lies are like their father that begets them—gross as a mountain, open, palpable.'

107. **Working so grossly in a natural cause:** operating together with such obvious fitness in carrying out the purposes to which they were both inclined by nature.

108. **admiration did not whoop at them:** wonder never cried out at them. The general thought is that nobody has ever been surprised at seeing murder and treason on the part of the same person, since they are natural associates, but that now at least it is astonishing that this particular traitor, Lord Scroop, should also be a murderer.

109. **'gainst all proportion:** contrary to all the fitness of things.

110. **to wait on:** to accompany.

112. **preposterously:** monstrously, against nature.

113. **Hath got the voice in hell for excellence:** has won for himself the vote of all the devils as being the best of them.

114. **suggest:** tempt.

115. **botch and bungle up damnation:** patch up a crime which deserves damnation with all sorts of pretenses to make it look virtuous.

116. **colours:** often used in the sense of 'pretext.'

118. **temper'd thee:** worked thee to his will, induced thee to commit this crime. *To temper* means 'to warm.' It is then often used for warming wax so that it can be moulded, and then in the sense of 'to mould,' as in this passage, figuratively.—**bade thee stand up:** abruptly ordered thee. 'Arise and go about this wicked business without affording me any pretext or excuses for so doing.'

119. **instance:** reason.

122. **with his lion gait walk the whole world.** A biblical figure. Cf. *1 Peter*, v, 8: 'Your adversary the devil, as a roaring lion, walketh about, seeking whom he may devour.'

123. **Tartar:** Tartarus, hell.

124. **legions.** Often used of companies of devils on account of the language of the Bible. Cf. *Mark*, v, 9: 'My name is Legion: for we are many.' The biblical tinge in this speech of the King's fits the sobriety of character with which he is described in this play. We are especially prepared for it by the words of the Archbishop of Canterbury in i, 1, 38–40:

> Hear him but reason in divinity,
> And, all-admiring, with an inward wish
> You would desire the King were made a prelate.

126. **jealousy:** suspicion.

127. **affiance:** allegiance, trust.—**Show:** appear.

128. **grave:** dignified, settled in character.

130. **religious.** The second *i* counts as a full syllable.

133. **swerving with the blood:** turning aside at every impulse.

134. **Garnish'd and deck'd in modest complement:** furnished with every appearance of moderation and self-control. *Complement* often means 'outward appearance.' In the phrase *modest complement* the order of ideas appears to be the opposite from that in modern English. This *modest complement* means 'the complement of modesty,' that is to say, 'the appearance of modesty.'

135. **Not working with the eye without the ear:** not acting rashly on the basis of what you see without some evidence that has come by ear.

136. **but in purged judgment trusting neither:** trust neither the evidence of the eye nor that of the ear except on the basis of well-tried and clarified consideration.

137. **so finely bolted:** of so fine (literally, so thoroughly sifted) a nature.

139. **full-fraught:** full freighted—i.e., fully furnished with all good qualities.—**indu'd:** endowed.

142. **Another fall of man.** Note the continuance of biblical phraseology in the King's speech.

144. **God acquit them of their practices!** God forgive them for their plots.

158. **prevention:** forestallment. In modern English any kind of hindrance may be called a *prevention*; in Elizabethan English the word was almost exclusively used for prevention by anticipation.

159. **in sufferance:** even while I am suffering death.—**rejoice:** rejoice at.

164. **Prevented.** See note on *prevention*, l. 158.

166. **God quit you:** the same as 'God acquit them' in l. 144.

169. **earnest:** partial payment in advance to bind the bargain.

175. **tender:** hold, regard.

181. **dear offences:** heinous offences. *Dear* is used of anything that affects one nearly, whether of love or hate, joy or sorrow.

188. **rub:** impediment. A figure from bowling.

190. **puissance:** powers, forces. Trisyllabic.

191. **in expedition.** The word implies not only expedition in the concrete sense, but also *haste*.

192. **the signs of war advance:** lift up the warlike standards. *Advance* in this sense is very common. Cf. *Tempest*, i, 2, 408: 'The fringed curtains of thine eyes advance,' meaning 'raise your eyelids; open your eyes.' Cf. also *Love's Labour's Lost*, iv, 3, 367; *Richard III*, v, 3, 265: 'advance your standards.'

193. **No king of England,** etc. This is the watchword of the King's foreign expedition.

Scene III.

An extraordinary scene—beyond question one of the most wonderful in Shakespeare. In mourning for Falstaff all these comic characters speak in accordance with their several whimsicalities of style and manner—Pistol rants, alliterates, and defies logic ('Bardolph, be blithe; . . . for Falstaff he is dead, And we must ern therefore'), the Hostess mixes up her words and speaks with ludicrous ambiguity, the Page pokes fun at Bardolph's nose and Bardolph resents it with his usual irascibility. Nothing could be more wildly comic than what is said; yet the general effect is that of almost unendurable pathos.

1. **bring:** accompany, escort.

3. **ern:** grieve.

10. **Arthur's bosom.** The Hostess confuses Abraham's bosom (*Luke*, xvi, 22) with the myth of King Arthur in the earthly paradise of Avalon.

11. **'A:** an abbreviated form of *he.*—**an:** as if.

12. **christom child:** the Hostess means 'child just christened.' Cf. Bunyan, *Life and Death of Mr. Badman* (ed. Dobrée, p. 268): '*Mr. Badman* died like a Lamb, or as they call it, like a *Chrisom* child, quietly and without fear.'

13. **the turning o' th' tide:** i.e., the moment when the time changes from night to day. *Tide* often means 'time' (which is, indeed, its original sense). Many think that *tide* is here used of the sea, and it is true that there is a belief that people die at ebb-tide rather than at flood. See B. Nicholson, in New Shakspere Society, *Transactions*, 1880–1886, pp. 212 ff.; Tusser, *Five Hundred Pointes of Good Husbandrie* (English Dialect Society ed.), p. 30.

14, 15. **fumble with the sheets.** Cf. Fletcher, *The Spanish Curate*, iv, 5, 47 (Variorum ed., II, 194): 'Do you see how he fumbles with the sheet?' Prosper Alpinus, *The Presages of Life and Death in Disease*, v, 14 (tr. by R. James, London, 1746, II, 85, 86): 'For the Hands and Feet to be moved and agitated after an odd and disorderly Manner, is condemned by *Hippocrates*, *Lib.* I. *Prognost.* where he says, "That they who under an acute Fever, Delirium, Peripneumony, or Cephalalgia, wave their Hands at every turn before their Face, or pick Motes, or pull Hairs out of the Clothes, or pick Straws from the Wall, are all in a bad and very dangerous State" '; Hippocrates, *Prognosticon*, in Karl Gottlob Kühn's *Medicorum Graecorum Opera*, xxi, 93 (also ed. W. H. S. Jones, II, 14):

ὁκόσοισιν ἐν πυρετοῖσιν ὀξέσιν . . . καὶ ἀποκαρφολογούσας, καὶ κροκίδας ἀπὸ τῶν ἱματίων ἀποτίλλούσας, καὶ ἀπὸ τοῦ τοίχου ἄχυρα ἀποσπώσας, πάσας εἶναι κακὰς καὶ θανατώδεας.

15. play with flowers: pick at the bedclothes, as if he were plucking flowers. Lodge names among 'signes to knowe if the patientt shall die'—'when his Nose waxethe sharpe'—'yf he picketh and gatherethe strawes' (*The Poore Man's Talentt*, 73, Hunterian Club ed.).

15, 16. smile upon his fingers' ends: Falstaff held up his fingers and smiled at them, imagining that he was looking at the flowers he had plucked.

16. but one way. Cf. Ford and Dekker, *The Witch of Edmonton*, iv, 2 (Ford, *Works*, ed. Gifford and Dyce, III, 253): 'there's no way with thee but one.'

17, 18. 'a babbled of green fields. It was because Falstaff talked of green fields in his delirium that the Hostess knew that he was 'playing with flowers.' Otherwise she would not have given this interpretation to his picking at the coverlet. This establishes, if any support is necessary, the correctness of Theobald's marvellous emendation of the Folio reading 'and a Table of green fields' to 'and 'a babbled of green fields.' Some have suggested that Falstaff was repeating bits of the Psalms,—'he maketh me to lie down in green pastures,'—but there is nothing to prove this, though of course of there is nothing impossible about it. It is simpler to suppose that he merely imagines himself roaming in the fields, a boy again. Superhuman efforts have been made by some scholars to avoid the acceptance of Theobald's emendation. Thus it has been proposed to read 'His nose was as sharp as a pen on a table of green field,' i.e., 'a table covered with green cloth,' the idea being that the sharpness of the quill pen would stand out on the green background. The reasons against this suggestion are obvious. In the first place, it is not (as is claimed by its advocates) a *conservative* reading. It departs from the Folio reading quite as much as Theobald's conjecture does, as anyone may see for himself by simply counting letters. In the second place, Dame Quickly's comparison is obviously proverbial,—'as sharp

as a pen,'—and the phrase should end there; the addition of 'on
a table,' etc., spoils the proverb and would be unnatural for her.
'On a table of green frieze' is even worse.[1] Theobald's reading
has been almost universally accepted as restoring perhaps the
most pathetic passage in all Shakespeare.

21. **should not think of God.** Cf. Marston, *The Dutch
Courtezan*, v, 3 (ed. Bullen, II, 100).

29. **of:** on, against.

39. **handle:** discuss.

40. **rheumatic:** the Hostess means 'lunatic,' 'delirious.'

47. **shog:** move on. Cf. ii, 1, 47.

50. **moveables:** furniture, etc. Note Pistol's proprietary air
—'*my* chattels.'

51. **Let senses rule:** let prudence govern (in the management of the tavern).—**Pitch:** plank down your money!—**Pitch
and pay.** Cf. Hazlitt, *Early Popular Poetry*, III, 288; Nashe, *The
Unfortunate Traveller* (*Works*, ed. McKerrow, II, 301, 302):
'The vintners, the brewers, the malt-men, and alewiues pray for
him. Pitch and pay, they will pray all day: score & borrow,
they will wish him much sorrow.'

54. **Hold-fast.** Cf. the proverb, 'Brag is a good dog, but
Hold-fast is better.'

55. **Caveto:** beware, be on your guard.

56. **clear thy crystals:** wipe your eyes. Cf. *Richard II*, i, 3,
208: 'the glasses of thine eyes'; *Coriolanus*, iii, 2, 117: 'the
glasses of my sight'; Kyd, *Spanish Tragedy*, ii, 5 (ed. Boas, 34):
'the glasses of his sight'; Studley, trans. *Hippolytus*, ii (Seneca,
Tenne Tragedies, Tudor Translations, I, 151): 'Those Cristall
Eyes'; *Garland of Good-Will*, Percy Society, xxx, 62: 'his crystal
eyes'; *Caesar's Revenge*, Malone Society, l. 423: 'by these chris-
tall eyes'; Greene, *The Carde of Fancie* (*Works*, ed. Grosart, IV,

[1]Green frieze is used to cover a counting board in the *Derby Accounts*
(ed. Lucy Toulmin Smith, p. 10, l. 5).

168): 'her Christal eyes'; Beaumont and Fletcher, *Philaster*, iii, 2, 48 (Variorum ed., I, 191): 'these crystals' [her eyes]; *The Custom of the Country*, i, 2, 48 (*ib.*, 500): 'her bright crystals'; *The Double Marriage* (ed. Waller, VI, 398): 'Sleep you sweet glasses, An everlasting slumber crown those Chrystals'; *Thierry and Theodoret*, v, 2 (ed. Dyce [2 vols.], i, 155): 'Love, I must die; I faint: Close up my glasses'; Ford, *Perkin Warbeck*, iv, 3 (ed. Gifford and Dyce, II, 190): 'Clear thy drown'd eyes'; *The Downfall of Robert Earl of Huntington*, iii, 1: 'Thy crystal eyes gaze in a crystal brook' (Collier's *Supplement* to Dodsley's *Old Plays*, 52); *A Match at Midnight*, iii, 1: 'that pair of chrystals' (Dodsley's *Old Plays*, ed. Collier, VII, 339); Lee, *Massacre of Paris*, v, 1 (1734 ed., III, 338): 'I'll gaze upon you till these Crystals run.'

57. **like horse-leeches.** Cf. *Proverbs*, xxx, 15: 'The horse-leech hath two daughters, crying "Give! give!"' Cf. Webster, *Duchess of Malfy*, i, 1, 54 (ed. Lucas, II, 38); Middleton, *The Family of Love*, ii, 3 (ed. Bullen, III, 33); Mabbe, *The Rogue* (Tudor Translations), IV, 298: 'Thus by little and little, like so many Horse-leeches, they went sucking all my bloud from me, till they had scarce left me one drop'; Pettie, *The Civile Conversation of M. Steeven Guazzo* (Tudor Translations), II, 161: 'The horseleach or bloud sucker, never leaves the flesh, untill she burst with fulnesse of bloud.'

63. **I cannot kiss.** The saturnine Nym has made up his quarrel with Pistol, but he cannot bring himself to kiss his lost love.

64. **Keep close:** live retired, don't go about. These prudent counsels from mine host Pistol are indescribably comic.

Scene IV.

1. **power:** forces.

7. **line:** strengthen, fortify.

10. **gulf:** whirlpool, maelstrom.

13. **the fatal and neglected English:** the fatally neglected English—hendiadys. The *late examples* are those of Crécy and Poictiers.

14. **redoubted:** feared. Cf. such expressions as *my dread lord*.

25. **Whitsun morris dance.** Whitsuntide was the time of spring festivities, among which the morris dance was conspicuous.

26. **so idly king'd:** furnished with so vain and empty-headed a king.

27. **so fantastically borne:** borne by so fantastic a creature, by such a fop or buffoon.

28. **humorous:** capricious, governed by whims and impulses.

34. **How modest in exception:** how moderate, self-controlled, in taking exception, or objecting.—**withal:** at the same time.

35. **constant:** firm.

36. **his vanities forespent:** his past follies.

37. **Brutus:** Brutus the Liberator, who pretended to be an idiot in order to remain unmolested by King Tarquin.

41. **Constable:** the chief military officer of France.

46. **of a weak and niggardly projection:** if they are planned on a feeble and niggardly scale.

47. **Doth.** The subject is the idea contained in what precedes —the fact that defensive measures are weakly planned.

50. **hath been flesh'd upon us:** hath been initiated in fighting against us, or hath been made fierce by feeding upon us.

51. **strain:** race, family.

54. **Cressy battle:** Edward the Third's victory over the French in 1346.—**struck:** fought.

57. **his mountain sire:** Edward III, born among the moun-

tains of Wales. Notice the repetition of the word. For this episode cf. *Edward III*, iii, 5, 1 ff.

67. present: immediate.

69, 70. coward dogs . . . threaten. Cf. Webster, *The White Devil*, iii, 2, 169 (ed. Lucas, I, 141): 'Cowardly dogs barke loudest.'

71. Good my sovereign. Note position of *good*.

75. England: the king of England.

83. the ordinance of times: ancient laws—especially the Salic Law.

85. sinister: literally, 'left-handed,' and so 'irregular,' with special allusion to the *bar sinister*, which is used in heraldry to denote illegitimate birth.—**awkward:** literally, 'back-handed,' and so 'indirect,' 'unlawful.'

88. line: pedigree.

89. demonstrative: proving his claim.

90. overlook: look over, examine.

91. evenly: in lawful and regular succession—opposed to *sinister* and *awkward* in l. 85.

94. indirectly: unjustly.

95. challenger: claimant.

101. That: so that.—**requiring:** request.

102. in the bowels of the Lord: by the compassion of the Lord. *In* is used in adjurations in the sense of 'by.' *Bowels* is a biblical word for 'mercy,' 'compassion.' Cf. *The First English Life of King Henry the Fifth* (ed. Kingsford, p. 32): 'wee exhorte you in the bowells of Jesus Christ'; Monstrelet, *Chroniques*, Paris, 1595, Vol. I, chap. 141, p. 223: 'Nous enhortons és entrailles de *Iesus-Christ*' (Henry V to Charles VI); Harsnet, *Declaration of Egregious Popish Impostures* (1603 ed., sig. A 2 v°): 'I beseech you in the bowels of our blessed Sauiour, to let open your eares & eyes to this short declaration.'

113. For us: for my part.

115. **For the Dauphin:** as for the Dauphin.

121. **at large:** in full.

124. **womby vaultages:** hollow caverns.

126. **second accent:** echo.—**ordinance:** ordnance.

129. **odds:** quarrel, controversy.

130. **vanity:** frivolity.

131. **Paris balls:** tennis balls.

133. **mistress court:** the chief court (a tennis term).

143. **footed:** landed.

145. **small breath:** small breathing space, short time for consideration.

ACT III. Prologue.

1. **imagin'd wing:** the wing of the imagination.

4. **well-appointed:** well-equipped.

5. **brave:** fine, handsome.

7. **Play with your fancies:** let your imagination act the play.

14. **rivage:** banks. The termination *-age* is collective. Cf. *sternage* in l. 18.

18. **sternage:** the sterns. See note on *rivage*, l. 14.

20. **with:** by.

21. **puissance:** strength.

24. **choice-drawn:** drawn by choice (not by lot), select.

32. **likes:** pleases.

33. **linstock:** the match, a bundle of combustibles on the end of a staff, with which old-fashioned cannon were set off. See cut on title page of Webbe's *Rare and Wonderfull Things*, in Ashbee's facsimiles, I.

33, stage direction. **Alarum:** call to arms (on a trumpet).—**chambers:** cannon.

Scene I.

9. **aspéct.** Regularly accented on the final syllable.

10. **portage:** portholes (the eyeholes). Cf. *rivage* (iii, Prologue, 14) and *sternage* (iii, Prologue, 18).

11. **o'erwhelm:** overhang. The action described is that of collecting the eyebrows and causing them to jut out in a terrific frown or scowl.

12. **galled:** worn (by the waves).

13. **confounded:** beaten by the sea; or, perhaps, submerged, swallowed up.

14. **Swill'd:** wasted.—**wasteful:** destructive, or barren (?).

16, 17. **bend up every spirit To his full height!** stretch every energy to its utmost power. The figure is from bending a bow or from winding up an engine of war (like a catapult or ballista) till it is on the stretch and ready to be discharged. Cf. *Macbeth* (i, 7, 79, 80):

> I am settled and bend up
> Each corporal agent to this terrible feat.

18. **fet:** fetched, derived.

21. **argument:** subject matter; and so, something to fight about (here practically = 'opposition').

27. **mettle:** quality (the same word as *metal*).

31. **slips:** leashes.

34. **'God for Harry! England and Saint George!'** The Folio punctuation ('God for Harry, England, and Saint George!') is absurd enough, but is followed by all editors. The proper punctuation was pointed out by Child.

35, stage direction. See note on iii, Prologue, 33, stage direction.

Scene II.

5. **a case of lives:** a *set* of lives—as we might say, 'nine lives like a cat.' *Case* is emphatic.

6. **plain-song:** the simple truth. *Plain-song* in music is the simple melody without variations or the like.

7. **just:** correct.—**humours.** Used very inexactly, in Pistol's fashion. He means that there are many 'queer things' happening.

19. **As duly, but not as truly:** i.e., you would hasten to London *duly* (as surely), but in so doing you would not be acting *truly* (as becomes a faithful subject).

21. **cullions:** rascals.

22. **men of mould:** men of earth, mortal men.

26. **bawcock:** my fine cock! A term of endearment, used only to men.—**chuck.** Another similar term, but of common gender. The absurdity of Pistol's applying these pet names to the fiery little Welshman who is driving him into the thick of the fight is obvious.

28. **These be good humours:** i.e., my friend Pistol has the right idea.—**wins bad humours:** i.e., acts in an unpleasant way. —With Nym *humour* means anything and everything.

29. Note the Boy's 'comic monologue.'

30. **swashers:** swashbucklers. The Boy's speech serves to instruct the audience as to the real character of Pistol and the rest. Such of the spectators as were not familiar with Shakespeare's *Henry IV* might need such information.

31, 32. **serve me:** enter into my service.

32. **man:** servant—with a pun on the other sense of man.

33. **antics:** buffoons. **For:** as for.

34. **white-liver'd:** cowardly.

35. **faces it out:** puts a good face on it.

37. **breaks words.** Pistol's mistakes in the use of words are notorious (cf. the phrase *broken English*).

39. **best men:** most courageous.

42. **broke:** to 'break one's head' is to draw blood on it—not, of course, to fracture one's skull.

45. **purchase:** booty, loot.

49. **that piece of service:** that warlike exploit.

49, 50. **carry coals:** a slang phrase for 'put up with insults or af-fronts.' Porters who carried coals were regarded as very low in-deed; hence the contemptuous use of the phrase. Cf. *Romeo and Juliet*, i, 1, 2: 'we'll not carry coals'; Cecil to Essex (in Sir Henry Ellis, *Original Letters Illustrative of English History*, III, 42): 'beare coales'; Marston, *Antonio's Revenge*, iv, 1 (ed. Bullen, I, 168): 'I would bear no coals'; Jonson, *Masque of Augurs* (ed. Morley, 293): 'this is not the first time you have carried coals'; Day, *Law Trickes* (ed. Bullen, p. 8): 'Ile carry coles and you will.'

51, 52. **handkerchers.** This form of the word was in good use in Shakespeare's time.

54, 55. **pocketing up of wrongs:** to bear an insult or injury without resenting it was called *pocketing it* or *putting it up*. The pun on *wrongs* is clear enough.

58. The presence of an English, a Welsh, a Scottish, and an Irish captain among the *dramatis personæ* makes the spirit of the play national in the largest sense. All English-speaking peoples in the British Isles send their fighting-men to aid the King. The intended moral for Shakespeare's times is clear enough.

58, 59. **presently:** immediately.

63, 64. **the disciplines of the war:** the principles of military science. Fluellen's hobby is Roman military theory.

65. **discuss:** report.—**is digt himself:** has dug (in his counter-mining operations).

68. **directions:** management.

70. **order:** conduct, arrangement.

77. **Roman.** Emphatic. Fluellen's idea is that only the Romans knew anything about military science. The subject is a mere fad (or 'humour') with him: he is not really a military antiquarian.

82, 83. **expedition:** Fluellen's error for 'experience.'

84, 85. **upon . . . directions:** I say this on the basis of my personal knowledge of his management.

89. **God-den:** good e'en—i.e., good evening (the regular greeting in the afternoon).

92. **pioners:** miners.—**given o'er:** given up the work.

93. Captain Macmorris's brogue is that of the Elizabethan stage Irishman. Doubtless it was as close to nature as is the case with the stage brogue to-day, but no closer. Other specimens may be seen in Dekker, *2 Honest Whore* (Pearson ed., II, 96) and *Old Fortunatus* (*ib.*, I, 152), and Ben Jonson's *Irish Masque.* In the *Life and Death of Captain Thomas Stukeley* (printed 1605) there is appended to a scene in Ireland in which there is no brogue another alternative scene in which the brogue is carried out to the extremest limit (Simpson, *School of Shakspere,* I, 192 ff.). Irishmen were well-known in London as chimney-sweeps and costermongers (Dekker, *2 Honest Whore,* Pearson ed., II, 96, 97). For Scotch, see Greene's *James IV.*

101, 102. **a few disputations:** a short discussion.

110. **quit you:** repay you—i.e., for the pleasure I take in hearing your debate.

111. **pick occasion:** find opportunity.

112. **It is no time to discourse.** Captain Macmorris is mortified and angry at the abandonment of the mining operations (of which he had been in charge) and is in no mood for formal discussion.

115. **beseech'd:** besieged.

130. **under your correction:** a courteous phrase—you will correct me if I am mistaken.

132. **Of my nation?** Macmorris is quick to suspect that Fluellen means to cast a slur on the Irish.

136. **Look you.** Fluellen keeps his temper with difficulty and grows very formal in the process.

146, 147. **you will mistake each other:** you insist on taking each other's words in an offensive sense when no offence is meant.

147. **that's a foul fault!** that's a bad error in logic. Cf. Beaumont and Fletcher, *The Mad Lover*, II, 3 (ed. Dyce [2 vols.], II, 20): 'that's a foul fault.'

151. **required:** Fluellen means 'found.'

Scene III.

2. **parle:** parley, conference.

4. **proud of destruction:** proudly bent on bringing destruction upon yourselves.

8. **half-achieved:** half-won. Cf. iv, 3, 91: 'Bid them achieve me, and then sell my bones,' and iii, 5, 60: 'For achievement, offer us his ransom.'

10. **The gates . . . up.** Cf. Day and Chettle, *The Blind Beggar of Bednall Green* (ed. Bang), l. 96: 'Sets open Mercies gate.'

11. **flesh'd:** made fierce by carnage. Cf. Howell, *Familiar Letters* (ed. Jacobs, I, 175, 176): '*Sultan Osman*, the *Grand Turke*, a Man according to the humour of that Nation, warlike and fleshed in blood, and a violent hater of *Christians*.'

17. **fell:** cruel, savage.

18. **Enlink'd to:** associated with.

30. **grace:** mercy.

31. **O'erblows:** blows away.—**filthy and contagious clouds.** Contagion was thought to reside in fogs and mists. The figure is eminently fitting, since one soldier 'catches' the spirit of riot and

butchery from another, until the whole army is infected. Cf. Dekker, *The Wonderfull Yeare* (Bodley Head Quartos), pp. 29, 30: 'vp rises a comfortable Sun out of the North, whose glorious beames (like a fan) dispersed all thick and contagious clowdes.'

32. **heady:** headstrong, impetuous.

46. **powers:** forces, troops.

50. **defensible:** capable of defending ourselves.

54. **For us:** as for me.

58. **addrest:** prepared, ready.

Scene V.

2. **withal:** with. Cf. l. 12.

5. **sprays:** offshoots.

6. **luxury:** lust.

11. **vië.** Dissyllabic.

12. **withal.** See note on l. 2.

13. **slobb'ry:** muddy.

14. **nook-shotten:** shot, or pushed, off into a corner of the earth. The French nobles regard England as a remote and barbarous island. Cf. *Cymbeline*, iii, 1, 12, 13: 'Britain is A world by itself'; *ib.*, iii, 4, 140–142: 'I' th' world's volume Our Britain seems as of it, but not in't; In a great pool a swan's nest'; *King John*, ii, 1, 29: 'that utmost corner of the West'; *As You Like It*, ii, 3, 42: 'unregarded age in corners thrown'; Catullus, xi, 12: 'ultimosque Britannos'; *ib.*, xxix, 4: 'Britannia ultima'; Horace, *Odes*, i, 35, 29 f.: 'in ultimos orbis Britannus'; *ib.*, iv, 14, 48: 'beluosus qui remotis obstrepit oceanus Britannis'; Virgil, *Ecl.*, i, 66; 'penitus toto divisos orbe Britannos'; Lyly, *Euphues* (ed. Croll and Clemons, p. 292): 'and had not England been thrust into a corner of the world'; Greene, *Friar Bacon and Friar Bungay*, ii, 1 (ed. Collins, II, 29): 'Welcome braue westerne

kings, To *Englands* shore, whose promontorie cleeues Shewes *Albion* is another little world'; Chapman, *The Masque of the Middle Temple, and Lincoln's Inn* (ed. Pearson, III, 103): 'This Ile is (for the excellency of it) diuided from the world (*diuisus ab orbe Britannus*)'; Rowley, *When You See Me, You Know Me* (1621 ed., sig. L v°): 'Wee dwell heere [*sic*], but in an outward Continent . . . Bordring vpon the frozen Orcades'; Dryden, *Astræa Redux*, l. 2: 'ours, a world divided from the rest'; *English Dialect Dictionary*, s.v. 'nook-shotten'; *Bye-Gones*, for 1907–1908, pp. 185, 201, 236; Wither, *History of the Pestilence* (ed. French, p. 9), makes God speak of the English thus:

> Is this the *Land* that wee haue lou'd soe long?
> And in our *Loue* elected from among
> The Heathen *Isles*, (wch at the first were hurl^d
> Into the vttmost corner of the world.

There is a wrong explanation by H. Cunningham in *The Times Literary Supplement*, June 29, 1933.

15. **batailles.** Trisyllabic.

17. **as in despite:** as if despising them.

18. **sodden:** boiled. The Constable refers to the national English beverage—ale.

19. **drench:** drink.—**sur-rein'd:** over-reined, exhausted by hard riding.—**jades:** a contemptuous term for 'horses.' Ale was often given to tired horses to refresh them.

20. **Decoct:** warm.

23. **roping:** hanging down like ropes.

26. **'Poor,'** etc. *Poor* is used to correct *rich*—our fields are rich in themselves, but they are poor with regard to the character of their owners.

29. **bred out:** exhausted by in-and-in breeding.

32. **bid us to:** bid us go to.

33. **lavoltas:** dances in which there was much jumping about.

—**corantos:** dances in which there was much rapid movement over the floor.

34. **grace:** excellence.

35. **lofty:** showy, high-mannered. There is a slight pause before *runaways*.

36. **Montjoy:** the official title of the chief herald of France.

37. **England:** the English king.

47. **seats:** fiefs—in return for which they were bound to fight for the king.—**quit you of:** redeem yourselves from.—**great.** Note repetition.

52. **spit and void his rheum upon.** Cf. *The Merchant of Venice*, i, 3, 118: 'You that did void your rheum upon my beard.'

53. **power:** forces.

59. **sink:** cesspool.

60. **for achievement,** etc.: instead of winning anything from us, will offer us ransom to allow him to go home. For *achieve* = 'get,' 'obtain,' cf. iii, 3, 8: 'the half-achieved Harflew'; and iv, 3, 91: 'Bid them achieve me, and then sell my bones.'

Scene VI.

4. **committed:** Fluellen's mistake for *performed*.

6. **magnanimous:** great-souled, valiant.

12. **discipline:** military science. Fluellen's fondness for military science and for the ancients appears on every occasion.

16. **estimation:** reputation.

17. **as gallant service:** such gallant service!

28. **buxom.** Perhaps Pistol means 'sturdy,' but it is idle to scrutinize very closely his peculiar use of language.

29–31. **Fortune's . . . wheel,** etc. Pistol has combined, in a deliciously inconsistent fashion, two conceptions of Fortune. In one of these her mutability is figured by a wheel (on which she

sometimes rides, as in Dürer's picture, and by which she sometimes sits and keeps it turning); in another she stands upon a
rolling stone. Cf. Kyd, *Cornelia*, i, ll. 102–106 (ed. Boas, p. 103):

> 'For we are proude, when Fortune fauours vs,
> As if inconstant Chaunce were alwaies one,
> Or, standing now, she would continue thus.
> O fooles, looke back and see the roling stone,
> Whereon she blindly lighting sets her foote';

and *The Spanish Tragedy*, i, 3 (*ib.*, p. 13): 'Fortune . . . Whose
foote [is] standing on a rowling stone.'

32. **By your patience,** etc. Fluellen cannot resist the tempta-
tion to read Pistol a little lecture on the emblems of Fortune.
He is not worried by the inconsistency of Pistol's combination.

42. **pax:** a little tablet, containing a relic, or a picture of
Christ, the Virgin, or a saint. The pax was kissed by the priest
at the mass, and then was passed about to be kissed by the
worshippers. Hence its name—from 'the kiss of *peace*.' Some
editors substitute *pyx*, the box or casket in which the host, or
consecrated wafer, is kept. But there is no need to make the
change. Indeed, *pax* is better than *pyx*, since a *pyx* was more
valuable than a pax, and Pistol emphasizes the small cost of the
article stolen. Cf. also what the Boy says of the petty thefts
committed by Bardolph and his comrades (iii, 2, 44 ff.). The
enormity of the offence would of course not be diminished by
the fact that the sacred object was intrinsically not very ex-
pensive, since the theft was sacrilege in any case. Cf. Thomas
Thacker to Cromwell (Ellis, *Original Letters*, Third Series, III,
107): 'Also that came from Seint Peters, a Crosse of siluer and
gilt, with Mary and John; a Pax of silver and gilt; a Pix of silver
and gilt'; *Paston Letters*, 1900, I, 490: 'Item, j. pax brede'; *The
Conflict of Conscience*, iii, 4 (*Hazlitt's Dodsley*, VI, 71); Greene,
The Blacke Booke's Messenger (*Works*, ed. Grosart, XI, 34–36);
The First English Life of King Henry the Fifth, ed. Kingsford,

p. 44: 'It was complayned to the Kinge a certaine Englishman in the hoast had violentlie taken from a Church a pixe of syluer . . . and the trespasser was ledd bounde as a thiefe thorough the hoast, and after hanged'; *The Archæological Journal*, LXI (1914), 120 ff.; H. J. Feasey, 'The Instrument of the Pax,' *The Antiquary*, XXXIII (1897), 209 ff.

44. Let gallows gape for dog. Cf. Heywood, *1 Edward IV*, iii, 1 (Shakespeare Society, p. 41):

> *Sellinger.* Then shalt thou be hanged.
> *Hobs.* A dog's death;

Fletcher, *Bonduca*, ii, 4 (ed. Waller, VI, 109): 'Hanging's a dog's death.'

47. little price: small value.

51. Speak. The Alexandrine, proper to the old style of tragedy, is appropriate in Pistol's dialect.

52. partly. Fluellen finds Pistol's strange English not altogether intelligible.

54. rejoice therefore. Addressed by Pistol to himself. He takes Fluellen's words as implying a favourable answer. There is a comic ambiguity in Pistol's exclamation, however, as if he were congratulating Fluellen on being able to understand him at all.

60. figo: a fig! As Pistol says this, he makes an insulting gesture, known as 'making the fig.' Cf. Shirley, *The Maid's Revenge*, i, 2 (ed. Gifford, I, 114), iii, 2 (*ib.*, p. 141); Shirley, *The Court Secret*, iv, 1 (*ib.*, v, 483): 'we have Spanish figs' [poisoned]; *The Noble Souldier* (Bullen's *Old Plays*, I, 331):

> *Queen.* Is't speeding? [an efficacious poison]
> *Mal[ateste].* As all our Spanish figs are.

Ford and Dekker, *The Sun's Darling*, iii, 1 (ed. Weber, II, 359; ed. Gifford and Dyce, III, 134); Nashe, *The Unfortunate Traveller* (ed. McKerrow, II, 299); Webster, *The White Devil*,

iv, 2 (ed. Lucas, I, 155; and see *ib.*, I, 240, II, 255, notes): 'I
doe looke now for a Spanish fig, or an Italian sallet daily'; *A
Warning for Fair Women* (ed. Simpson, II, 258): 'Tut, a fig's end';
J. O. Halliwell (ed.), *The Marriage of Wit and Wisdom*, etc.,
Shakespeare Society, p. 107; New Shakspere Society, *Transactions*, 1880–1885, p. 400; *Zeitschrift für den Deutschen Unter-
richt*, V, 107 (note), VI, 53, VII, 491, 570; *Germania* (ed. F. H.
von der Hagen), VII (1846), 183 ff.; Otto John, 'Über den
Aberglauben des bösen Blicks bei den Alten,' in K. Sächsische
Gesellschaft der Wissenschaften zu Leipsig, *Berichte über Ver-
handlungen*, VII (1850), 80; Wier, *De Praestigiis Daemonum*
(1568), p. 597.

61. **It is well.** Said with awful calmness, which Pistol is un-
lucky enough to mistake for cowardice.

62. **The fig of Spain!** Pistol repeats the gesture. He says the
'fig of Spain!' since the sign in question was used by Spaniards.
Cf. 'Do this, and fig me, like The bragging Spaniard' (*2 Henry IV*,
v, 3, 123, 124). A discussion of 'making the fig' may be found in
Douce's *Illustrations of Shakspere*, pp. 302 ff.

65. **bawd:** pander.

66. **prave:** brave—i.e., fine.

69. **is serve:** Fluellen's mistake for 'shall serve.'

70. **gull:** properly, dupe; but often used for 'foolish fellow'
in general.

74. **learn:** teach.

76, 77. **sconce:** breastwork.—**convoy:** the guarding of a pro-
vision train.

77. **bravely:** with credit.

78. **stood on:** insisted on.

79, 80. **new-tuned:** novel-sounding. The figure comes, of
course, from the affectation of knowing all the latest and most
fashionable songs.

84. **slanders of the age:** persons who are a disgrace to the times.

85. mistook. As Fluellen has been in the present case by taking Pistol for a brave soldier.

87, 88. hole in his coat: something discreditable in his record. **—my mind:** what I think of him.

91. speak . . . pridge: tell him the news I have brought from the bridge; or, perhaps, speak *concerning* the bridge.

98. passages: acts, deeds.

103. perdition: loss.

104. reasonable. Fluellen uses this word as if it were stronger than *very*, as of course it is not.

108. bubukles: carbuncles.

113. We would, etc. The King's ignoring of his former familiarity with Bardolph is grim testimony to his reformation.

121. habit: i.e., his herald's attire.

122. of: from.

127. Advantage: caution (a considerate waiting for an advantageous opportunity).

130. bruise: squeeze. The figure is from the treatment of a boil or the like. Cf. *King John*, iv, 2, 79–81.

131. upon our cue: i.e., now the proper moment has come for us to speak. A common theatrical figure.

133. admire our sufferance: wonder at my patience.

136, 137. digested: put up with. For the figure see note on 'well digest Th' abuse of distance' (ii, Prologue, 31). The very words of the King's defiance are a confession of the disgraces he has suffered.

137. in weight to re-answer: to make full compensation for. Note that *compensate* means literally 'to *weigh* with.'

139. the muster of his kingdom: the whole population of England. *Muster* is practically equivalent to 'census.'

146. quality: rank and profession (as chief herald of France).

148. fairly: handsomely.

151. impeachment: hindrance.

153. **an enemy of craft and vantage:** a crafty enemy who is stronger than one's self.

161. **in:** into.

163. **trunk:** the only ransom he will offer is his own body, which the French king may have *if he can get it.*

165. **God before.** See i, 2, 307, and note.

167. **There's for thy labour.** He gives the herald a purse or a jewel.

181. **bid them march away:** give orders to our army to march towards Calais.

Scene VII.

---

1 ff. This frivolous scene is in accordance with what history tells us of the demeanour of the French on the eve of the battle.

13. **pasterns:** the pastern is part of a horse's foot between the fetlock and the hoof.

14. **as if his entrails were hairs:** as if he were a tennis ball, stuffed with hair.

15. **avec.** *Chez* (see Textual Notes) makes no sense, since it cannot be taken as 'with' unless we ascribe to Shakespeare a kind of ignorance of French which is inconceivable. The emendation *qui a* may be accepted.

18. **basest horn of his hoof:** the lowest note which his horny hoof sounds as it strikes the earth.

22. **Perseus:** who rode through the air on Pegasus.

26. **jades:** a disrespectful term for 'horses.'

27. **absolute:** perfect.

32. **No more.** Orleans is bored by the Dauphin's extravagant boasting.

35. **vary deserved praise:** utter praise in many variations, all of it well-deserved.

37. **argument:** subject.

38. **reason:** discourse.

49. **Me.** Emphatic.—**prescript:** special and appropriate.

50. **particular:** who is one's very own.

68. **Le chien,** etc. Cf. *2 Peter*, ii, 29: 'The dog is turned to his own vomit again; and the sow that was washed to her wallowing in the mire.'

78. **my sky.** He means that there will still be stars enough in the sky of his *honour*.

80. **'twere mere honour:** i.e., your armour is too new; you have never had any of the spangles on it knocked off in battle.

90. **fac'd out of my way:** browbeaten so as to abandon my course. An obvious pun.

93, 94. **go to hazard . . . for twenty prisoners:** play at hazard (a game at dice) with twenty English prisoners as the stake.

103. **tread out the oath:** the idea is that the lady may fulfil the oath by dancing, since the Dauphin is more likely to distinguish himself in that way than in the battle.

121, 122. **hooded . . . bate.** Falconing terms. The falcon was often carried with a hood over its head; and when this was removed, the bird was likely to *bate*, i.e., 'to flap the wings' (French *battre*). *Bate* also means 'to abate,' and in that sense is applied to the Dauphin's valour, which is likely to diminish when the time to show it actually comes.

123. **Ill will,** etc. The rest of this conversation is an example of the common diversion of 'capping proverbs,'—answering one proverb by another,—the person who has the last word being the winner. One of the best examples of this sport is the following sonnet by Michael Drayton (lix):

> As Love and I, late harbour'd in one inn,
> With proverbs thus each other entertain:
> "In love there is no lack," thus I begin,
> "Fair words make fools," replieth he again;
> "Who spares to speak, doth spare to speed" (quoth I)
> "As well" (saith he) "too forward, as too slow:"

> "Fortune assists the boldest," I reply,
> "A hasty man" (quoth he) "ne'er wanted woe:"
> "Labour is light, where love" (quoth I) "doth pay,"
> (Saith he) "Light burthens heavy, if far borne:"
> (Quoth I) "The main lost, cast the by away,"
> "Y' have spun a fair thread," he replies in scorn.
> And having thus awhile each other thwarted,
> Fools as we met, so fools again we parted.

Cf. *Wealth and Health*, Malone Society, l. 840: 'ylwyl cannot say wel.' For a proverb contest, see Porter, *The Two Angry Women of Abington* (ed. Gayley, pp. 566 ff.).

134. **you were overshot.** Cf. R. B. Merriman, *Life and Letters of Thomas Cromwell*, II, 44: 'ye are far ouershotte [mistaken] in that behalf'; Chapman, *The Gentleman Usher*, i, 2 (Pearson ed., I, 264; ed. Parrott, 242): 'There y'are overshot'; *The Birth of Merlin*, ii, 1 (ed. Brooke, *Shakespeare Apocrypha*, p. 358): 'you have been fouly o'reshot'; Thomas Russell (ed.), *Works of Tyndale and Frith*, III, 34: 'Belike the man had there over shot himself foul'; John Morris, *Troubles of our Catholic Forefathers*, I, 100: 'Very much surely was Mr. Manwood overshot, and through the black mist of malice blinded'; [John Weever,] *The Mirror of Martyrs* (1601), in H. H. Gibbs (ed.), *The Hystory of the Moste Noble Knight Plasidas*, 201: 'Grieu'd at the world, in anger ouer-shot, My iust complaint I almost had forgot.'

142. **peevish:** childish, foolish.

143, 144. **to mope:** to come blundering along, like a man walking in his sleep.—**fat-brain'd:** stupid.

144. **so far out of his knowledge:** so far away from any region with which he is acquainted. Orleans's comparison is that of a stupid fellow who blunders into a strange region and loses his way. Cf. Defoe, *Captain Singleton*: 'William . . . told them a fair story enough, that the ship was in scarcity of provisions, that they were driven a great way out of their own, and indeed, as we say, out of their knowledge' (*Works*, ed. Maynadier, VI, 220).

145. apprehension: common sense—not, fear. The idea is that they are too stupid to know the danger they are in.

153. winking: with their eyes shut—i.e., with blind and stupid courage.

154. a Russian bear. The reference is, of course, to bear-baiting, for which purpose Russian bears were much esteemed.

158. Just, just! exactly so.—**do sympathize with:** resemble, are like. *Sympathy* is often used of agreement or correspondence.

159, 160. robustious: boisterous.[1]—**coming on:** making an attack on, assault.

163. shrowdly: deucedly. —**out of beef.** Cf. *Edward III*, iii, 3, 159 (ed. Brooke, *Shakespeare Apocrypha*, p. 87):

> Scant them of their chines of beefe
> And take awaie their downie featherbedes
> And presently they are as resty stiffe,
> As twere a many ouer ridden iades';

The Play of Stucley (ed. Simpson, *The School of Shakespeare*, i, 192):

> These English churls die if they lack their bed
> And bread and beer, porridge, and powdered beef.

166. stomachs to eat and none to fight. A common pun.

---

[1]Cf. *Hamlet*, iii, 2, 10; Nashe, *Lenten Stuff* (ed. McKerrow, III, 191): 'harden his soft bleding vaines as stiffe and robustious as branches of Corrall'; Drayton, *Polyolbion*, Song I (ed. Chalmers, p. 172 b); Daniel, *Hymen's Triumph*, ii, 1 (ed. Grosart, III, 353): 'my robustious manly ancestours'; Milton, *Eikonoklastes*, chap. 4 (Bohn ed., I, 349): 'they had handled the bishops in a more robustious manner'; Francis Kirkman, *The English Rogue*, London, 1671, p. 51: 'Now I going out of the door first, one of these robustious fellows [catchpoles] laid hands upon me.'

Act IV. Prologue.

1. **entertain conjecture:** receive into your minds an idea. The phrase is practically equivalent to 'imagine.'

2. **poring dark.** The epithet *poring* is transferred from the person to the thing. The *poring dark* is the dark which makes anybody pore, or look closely, in order to see anything.

4. **foul.** Because black.

6. **That:** so that.

9. **battle:** host.—**umber'd:** brown or yellowish—on account of the play of firelight on their faces. Cf. Heywood, *The Captives*, ii, 2 (ed. Bullen, *Old Plays*, IV, 148): 'lyke gypsies umber'd.'

12. **accomplishing:** finishing—i.e., putting the finishing touches to their armour.

17. **secure:** free from care.

18. **over-lusty:** over-merry.

19. **low-rated:** undervalued.

25. **gesture sad:** sober bearing.

26. **Investing:** clothing. The figure is a favourite one with Shakespeare. Here the sober bearing of the men is spoken of as clothing their cheeks and coats, inasmuch as one's bearing is in a certain sense the garment which covers everything. Cf. *Edward III*, iv, 5, 36 (ed. Brooke, *Shakespeare Apocrypha*, p. 95):

> In briefe, our souldiers haue let fall their armes,
> And stand like metamorphosd images,
> Bloudlesse and pale, one gazing on another.

33. **good morrow:** good morning.

35. **note:** indication.

37. **dedicate one jot of colour,** etc.: he does not lose any of his freshness of complexion on account of the fact that he has been awake all night.

38. **all-watched night:** the night in which he has not slept at all.

39. **freshly looks:** looks fresh. The adverb was regular in Elizabethan English.—**overbears attaint:** conquers the natural fagged appearance which one has who has not slept.

41. **That:** so that.

45. **mean and gentle all.** This may be either the vocative, addressed to the audience in the theatre, or the nominative (the subject of *behold*), referring to the soldiers in the English army. The vocative construction is more probable, since the Chorus is giving an account of the scenes that are to come. *Mean* was not an offensive word. It simply meant 'persons of low degree.'

46. **as may unworthiness define:** so far as our poor and un-worthy abilities can depict it.

47. **A little touch of Harry in the night:** a scene which shall give some slight idea of his conduct as he goes about the camp.

48. **And so:** i.e., after we have presented the scene which gives 'A little touch of Harry in the night.'

49. **(O for pity!)** A mere ejaculation like 'Alas! a pity!' or 'What a pity!'

50. **foils:** persons armed with foils. Properly *foils* were blunted swords used in fencing; here the term is used con-temptuously for the swords which the players carry.

51. **Right ill-dispos'd:** very ill-arranged.

52. **Yet:** despite the poorness of our representation.

53. **Minding true things,** etc.: seeing in our mind's eye the actual facts on the basis of the imitations which we present.

Scene I.

---

1 ff. In the scene that follows—'the little touch of Harry in the night'—the King has an interview with almost every kind of person in the host. First with a great noble, Gloucester; next with Sir Thomas Erpingham, a sturdy and honourable old knight; then with the rascally and boasting Pistol; again with

Fluellen and Gower, two captains equally devoted to him, but of a different race; last of all, with the sturdy English private soldiers, Bates, who represents the good-natured and easy-going Englishman, and Williams, who is a fine example of the national habit of grumbling, in which John Bull has always taken a certain pride.

4. **some soul of goodness:** some kernel or nucleus of goodness.

7. **Which is both healthful, and good husbandry.** Cf. the rhyme:

> Early to bed and early to rise
> Makes a man healthy, wealthy, and wise.

Husbandry means 'thrift,' 'economy.' The King's observation covers two of Poor Richard's trio of advantages. Cf. *Pericles*, iii, 2, 20.

8. **our outward consciences:** they serve us in place of conscience, though they are external to us and not within, as consciences are.

10. **dress us fairly:** make ourselves well prepared.

14 ff. **good soft pillow**, etc. This remark, with Erpingham's answer, is historical.

15. **a churlish turf:** *churlish* means 'niggardly.' The French turf begrudges Erpingham a good night's sleep.

16. **likes me:** pleases me.

19. **Upon example:** for example, on account of example— i.e., by remembering some other person who endures the like.

21. **defunct and dead:** these two words mean practically the same thing—'paralyzed,' as it were.

23. **casted slough.** The figure is from a snake which casts its skin.—**legerity:** nimbleness, vigour.

25. **Commend me:** give my regards.

26. **Do my good morrow to them:** bid them good morrow in my name.

34. God-a-mercy: gramercy, many thanks. *Gramercy* is a corruption of *graunt mercy*, i.e., 'great thanks.' *God-a-mercy*, which properly means 'God have mercy,' has been confused with this phrase.

37. Discuss unto me: tell me.

38. popular: one of the common people.

39. a gentleman of a company: an inferior officer, a non-commissioned officer. Cf. Heywood, *The Four Prentices of London* (Pearson ed., II, 173): 'All Commanders, Captaines, Liefetenants, Gentlemen of Companies, Sergeants, Corporals, or common Souldiers whatsoeuer'; Earle, 'Younger Brother,' *Microcosmographie* (ed. Arber, p. 30): 'His last refuge is the Low-countries, where rags and lice are no scandall, where he liues a poore Gentleman of a Company, and dies without a shirt'; Shirley, *The Young Admiral*, ii, 1 (ed. Gifford and Dyce, II, pp. 127, 128, 130); Judges, *The Elizabethan Underworld*, 259; Arber, *English Garner*, I (1877), p. 463; Massinger, *The Maid of Honour*, iii, 1 (ed. Hartley Coleridge, p. 199; ed. Gifford, III, 51); Beaumont and Fletcher, *The Honest Man's Fortune*, ii, 2 (ed. Dyce [2 vols.], I, 529): 'I myself was but then gentleman of a company'; Clifford Walton, *History of the British Standing Army from 1660 to 1700*, pp. 415, 416: 'The Gentleman of a Company was a soldier on probation for promotion, and as such he acted as file-leader, was placed on centry over posts of trust or responsibility, and occasionally drilled a squad of his own file: in fact he was a lance-corporal on probation.'

44. bawcock: fine fellow. A term used exclusively of men. Literally, fine cock. See iii, 2, 26.—**a heart of gold.** Cf. *Thersytes*, in *Four Old Plays* (ed. Child, 62): 'What saie you hart of gold?'

45. A lad of life: a lively lad.—**an imp of fame:** *imp* means 'scion,' and is often used for a young person. Hence *imp of fame* means 'a scion of a famous stock.'

48. bully: a slang term of endearment.

51. a Welshman. The King was born at Monmouth, in Wales.

54. his leek. See *The Cambrian Journal*, I (1854), 190, 372.

59. his kinsman. The Welsh were famous for keeping their genealogical connections up to the remotest degree. Hence it is proverbial that all Welsh gentlemen are related.

60. The figo for thee. See note on iii, 6, 60.

61. God be with you! i.e., good-bye.

63. sorts well with: well befits.

65. So! yes, I am he.—**speak lower.** Gower has hailed Fluellen in a loud voice on meeting him suddenly in the dark.

66. admiration: wonder.

67, 68. prerogatifes: used here in the same sense as 'laws' or 'rules.'

71. Tiddle taddle: tittle tattle.—**pibble pabble.** Cf. Hazlitt, *Early Popular Poetry*, IV, 130: 'alwaies they [women] bible bable'; 'An Interlocucyon betwyxt Man and Woman,' in Guillaume Alexis, *Œuvres Poétiques* (ed. Piaget and Picot, i, 151): 'ye togyther byb, chatrying lyke a pye'; *Ballads from Manuscripts* (ed. Furnivall, I, 264): 'With bible and bable'; Heywood, *The Spider and the Flie* (Spenser Society ed., p. 294): 'all confused so, in such bibble babble'; *ib.*, 387: 'in all this bybble babble.'

72. Pompey's camp. Fluellen's example is unfortunate, inasmuch as Pompey's most famous camp, that just before the Battle of Pharsalia, was noted for its luxury and lack of discipline. No doubt Shakespeare knew this from his Plutarch, and intentionally makes Fluellen's learning go astray.

75. modesty: moderation—the same as 'sobriety.'

82. I will speak lower. Gower is convinced of the wisdom of Fluellen's words.

85. a little out of fashion: a little quaint.

86. care: carefulness. Fluellen's valour is well-known. His caution is shown in the preceding conversation which the King has overheard.

89. **I think it be.** This use of the subjunctive in indirect discourse is not meant to imply any particular doubt. Cf. *Othello*, iii, 3, 385: 'I think my wife be honest, and think she is not.'

99. **estate:** state, condition.

100. **a sand:** a sand bar.

107. **the element:** the sky.—**shows:** appears, looks.

108, 109. **conditions:** characters, qualities.

109. **ceremonies:** his clothes of state, his splendid apparel.

110, 111. **affections:** feelings.

111. **are higher mounted:** soar higher.

112. **stoop:** descend in their flight.—**with the like wing:** in the same way, in similar flight. The language of this metaphor is taken from the technical vocabulary of falconry.

114. **out of doubt:** beyond question.—**be of the same relish:** taste the same way to him—i.e., when the King feels, his feeling is like ours, though when he hopes, his hopes may be higher than ours.

115, 116. **no man should possess him with any appearance of fear:** no man should put the King in possession of (i.e., let the King see) any appearance of fear in him.

121, 122. **at all adventures:** at all hazards. Bates means that he would take the risk of being in the Thames up to the neck rather than the risk of being in his present situation.

123, 124. **my conscience:** what I really think.

129. **to wish:** as to wish.

133. **his cause being just,** etc. The King's confidence in the justice of his cause is insisted on with good effect here. Our minds revert to the elaborate discussion of this question at the beginning of the play.—**quarrel:** the cause for which one contends.

143. **the latter day:** the day of judgment.

144, 145. **some swearing,** etc.: i.e., the owners of the legs and arms referred to.

145. **some upon their wives:** i.e., some crying out upon their wives. *To cry out upon* sometimes means 'to cry out against' and sometimes, as here, merely 'to mention by way of lamentation or regret.'

147. **rawly left:** left in poor circumstances. *Raw* means 'not provided for.' We have the same use of the word in *Macbeth*, iv, 1, 26: 'Why in that rawness left you wife and child?' i.e., why did you leave your wife and children in so unprepared and defenceless a state? Note that the adverb *rawly* is precisely equivalent to 'in rawness.' The use of an adverb in *-ly* to express condition rather than manner is common. Cf. *Merchant of Venice*, i, 1, 161: 'In Belmont is a lady richly left,' i.e., left rich by her father at his death. Cf. Merriman, *Life and Letters of Thomas Cromwell*, II, 102: 'I haue not seen a wise man leave his thinges soo rawlye, as yours be left.'

148. **afeared.** Now rustic, but not so then.—**die well:** i.e., make a good end, die a Christian death.

149, 150. **charitably dispose of anything:** make such a disposition of their affairs as accords with Christian charity—i.e., forgive enemies, etc.

150. **argument:** the whole subject of their thoughts at the time.

153. **all proportion of subjection:** all propriety or reason on the part of his subjects.

154. **So:** i.e., on the principle that Williams has just laid down. Williams's arguments are common and would instantly appeal to the rank and file in the Elizabethan theatre. The King's computation of fame is a good example of his ability to reason in morality and justifies the opinion pronounced on him by the Archbishop of Canterbury in the first act.—**sent about merchandise:** sent on a trading voyage.

155. **do sinfully miscarry upon the sea:** is lost at sea while in a state of sin. Cf. the note on *rawly* in l. 147. *Miscarry* is a common euphemism for 'meet with a fatal accident.'

160, 161. in many irreconcil'd iniquities: with many sins upon his conscience for which he has not made his peace with God.

163, 164. to answer the particular endings of his soldiers: to be responsible for the particular way in which each of his soldiers meets his death—i.e., whether in a condition of harmony with God or the reverse.

166. they: i.e., the king, the father, the master.

169. arbitrement: judgment, decision.

169, 170. all unspotted soldiers: with soldiers, none of whom shall be stained with guilt.

173. the broken seals of perjury: perjury itself is the act of breaking the seal of an oath.

173, 174. making the wars their bulwark: hiding behind the defence of warfare. Taking advantage, in other words, of a war-like time, these soldiers have inflicted injury on non-combatants or peaceable citizens.

176, 177. outrun native punishment: escaped punishment in their native land.

179. beadle: an officer whose duty it is to arrest and punish for various offences.

184. unprovided: unprepared for death.

187. visited: visited with God's vengeance, punished.— **Every subject's duty is the King's:** the King has a right to the duty of every subject.

189. mote: least spot—a manifest allusion to the parable of the mote and the beam.

190. dying so: i.e., dying with a clean conscience.

194. making God so free an offer: since he offered his soul so freely to the Lord.

197. 'Tis certain, etc. Williams is convinced by the King's logic and sums up the argument in complete assent with him.

201. lustily: vigorously.

204. Ay, he said so, etc. Williams is a fine specimen of the sturdy, grumbling Englishman. His national characteristic of finding fault must not deceive anybody as to his loyalty, which is substantial.

209. **You pay him then!** Said very sarcastically—'That will be a terrible punishment for him, won't it!'

210. **an elder-gun:** a pop-gun made out of an elder stick with the pith taken out. Cf. Beaumont and Fletcher, *Philaster*, i, 1, 265 (Variorum ed., I, 147): 'upon the report of an elder-gun.'

212. **go about:** undertake.

216. **round:** outspoken, blunt.

218. **convenient:** fitting.

223. **gage:** pledge.

224. **bonnet:** cap.

231. **take:** give.

240. **enow:** enough. Often used as a plural, but not exclusively so.

242. **lay:** bet. The pun on *crowns* is obvious.

245. **to cut French crowns:** the two senses are (1) to clip the coins known as French crowns; (2) to cut French heads with the sword.

246. **a clippen.** This carries out the pun. A person who cut off small pieces of coin so as to make them under weight was called a clipper. The punishment for this was death. It was easy to clip coins in old times, because they were not exactly round and had not milled edges as at the present day.

247 ff. With this soliloquy cf. Seneca, *Hercules Œtæus*, ii, Chorus (Tudor Translations ed., II, 216).

248. **careful:** anxious.

251. **subject.** This agrees with *greatness*. Majesty itself is subject to the foolish talk of everybody.

252. **sense:** sensibility, sensitiveness.

253. **his own wringing:** that which pinches him. *To wring* was 'to pinch' or 'to twist.' There is doubtless an allusion to the

old proverb 'I know best myself where my shoe wrings me,' or, as we say now, 'where the shoe pinches.'—**heart's-ease:** a beautiful old word for 'contentment.'

254. **neglect:** disregard, pass by, do without—not implying any culpability, as is the case to-day with the word.

256. **ceremony:** used in the most general sense for 'pomp and all that attends rank.'

260. **comings-in:** income.

262. **thy soul of adoration:** that essential quality which makes thee so much adored.

268. **great greatness.** The repetition, like plays on words in general, here expresses contempt.

271. **blown.** Words are but breath, and breath is but air; hence it is common to find all sorts of words appropriate to wind used of speech.

272. **give place to:** give way to, retire before.—**flexure:** means the same thing as 'low bending.' Cf. *No-Body and Some-Body*, l. 1062 (Simpson, *The School of Shakespeare*, I, 318): 'There's those are made For flexure, let them stoope.'

274. **thou proud dream.** The King is still apostrophizing ceremony.

275. **play'st so subtilly with a king's repose:** cheats a king so cleverly out of his repose.

276. **find thee:** find thee out, detect thy real nature.

277. **balm:** i.e., the holy oil with which kings are anointed at their coronation.—**the ball:** i.e., the apple or globe, a figure of universal sovereignty.

279. **The intertissued robe of gold and pearl:** the coronation mantle interwoven with gold and pearls.

280. **The farced title:** the stuffed title; hence, the long and elaborate title. The word *farced* expresses contempt. The title is said to run before the king by a lively figure. Just as the person who announces the coming of the king runs before him

to clear the way, so the title may be said to precede the king wherever he goes.

281. **the tide of pomp:** i.e., the flood tide of splendid ceremony.

283, 284. Note the variation of accent in the phrase *all these*. This accords with a common trick of Elizabethan metre.

284 ff. Note the similarity of Henry V's reflection on sleep to that of his father in *2 Henry IV*, iii, 1.

286. **vacant:** free from care.

287. **distressful bread:** bread gained by hard labour.

292. **Hyperion:** the sun. In order to help Hyperion harness his horses one must, of course, rise before dawn. Cf. Greene, *Alphonsus, King of Arragon*, iv, 2 (ed. Collins, I, 116): 'Hyperions coach.'

296. **Winding up:** occupying and closing.—**nights with sleep:** Cf. *The Misfortunes of Arthur*, iii, 4 (ed. Grumbine, p. 166):

> Behold, the Peasant poore with tattered coate,
> Whose eyes a meaner *Fortune* feedes with sleepe,
> How safe and sound the carelesse Snudge doth snore.

297. **forehand:** advantage. *Vantage* in the same line is a synonym.

298. **a member of the country's peace:** i.e., a person who belongs to a peaceable and well-ordered community.

299. **it:** i.e., the peace which the king maintains.—**gross:** stupid.—**wots:** knows.

301. **Whose hours the peasant best advantages.** *Advantages*, though in the singular, seems to have *hours* for its subject and *peasant* for its object. The usual meaning of *vantage*, when a verb, is 'to profit,' 'to be for the advantage of.' It is conceivable, however, that *peasant* is the subject and *hours* the object, in which case *hours* must be taken as meaning 'gets the profit of,' 'profits by.' To have a plural noun and a singular verb was very common in Elizabethan English.

302. **jealous of your absence:** suspecting, because of your absence, that some harm has come to you. *Jealous* regularly = 'suspicious.'

305. **I shall do't.** The most courteous form of assent in Elizabethan English was *I shall* rather than *I will*, because *I shall* suggests that obedience is *inevitable*, a matter of course, and not dependent on the speaker's volition.

306. What follows shows the King in a devout mood and completes the 'little touch of Harry in the night.'

308. **The sense of reck'ning:** the ability to count or reckon.

310, 311. **the fault My father made.** *To make a fault* was a regular Elizabethan idiom, from the French *faire une faute*. The murder of Richard II is meant.

311. **compassing:** getting possession of.

318. **chantries:** chapels for the performance of special masses for the souls of the dead. They were usually attached to a cathedral church.

319. **still:** ever, without ceasing.

320. **Do.** Emphatic. He means that no mere actions can expiate the guilt of Richard's murder, since, when he has done everything that is possible, he feels that he must still add his penitent prayer to God to forgive his father's crime, the guilt of which seems in a manner to descend to him.

Scene II.

This scene is merely the conclusion of the last scene in Act III. The day, so longed for by the French nobles, has dawned at last.

1. **Up:** not 'rise from sleep,' of course, but 'to horse.'

2. **Varlet:** valet. The same as *laquais*, 'lackey.'

4. **Via!** on!

10. **in:** into.

11. **dout them:** put them (the eyes) out (from *do out*; like *don* from *do on*, *doff* from *do off*, *dup* from *do up*).—**with super-fluous courage:** with the blood which they have in greater abundance than is necessary. Courage and fullness of blood were thought to go together. The horses, having a superabundance of courage, may well spare some of their blood.

14. **embattail'd:** drawn up in battle array.

17. **fair show:** gallant appearance.

21. **curtleaxe:** cutlass.

25. **'Tis positive 'gainst all exceptions:** it may be asserted positively in defiance of all objection or contradiction. Cf. the phrase *to take exception* for 'to object.'

28. **enow:** enough. Often plural, though not always.

29. **hilding:** wretched, insignificant. Used either as a noun or as an adjective.

31. **speculation:** looking on.

35. **tucket sonance.** G[ervaise] M[arkham] in *The Souldier's Accident* mentions as one of the 'Sounds and Commands of the Trumpet,' for cavalry, the '*Tucquet*,—or—March' (New Shak-spere Society, *Transactions*, 1880–1885, Part II, p. 86).

36. **dare:** frighten. Cf. *to dare larks*.[1]

37. **couch:** crouch.

39. **desperate of their bones:** without hope of saving them-selves, poor skeletons that they are.

40. **Ill-favouredly,** etc.: i.e., these scarecrows are a disfigure-ment to the fair landscape and ought to be cleared away.

42. **passing:** surpassingly, very.

43. **Big:** threatening. The idea is that they look like a troop of military bankrupts—so poverty-stricken is their appearance.

---

[1]Cf. *Greenes Never Too Late* (*Works*, ed. Grosart, VIII, 25): 'that set out their faces as Foulers doe their daring glasses, that the Larkes that soare highest, may stoope soonest'; *Anglia*, XIII, 467, note; Heywood, *The Spider and the Flie*, cap. 24, st. 4.

44. **beaver:** the moveable part of the helmet.

45. **candlesticks:** ornamental candlesticks, etc., often had the form of horsemen, lance in hand. Cf. Webster, *The White Devil*, iii, 1 (ed. Dyce, p. 19; ed. Lucas, I, 136): 'he showed like a pewter candlestick, fashioned like a man in armour, holding a tilting-staff in his hand, little bigger than a candle of twelve i' the pound.'

46. **jades:** a contemptuous term for 'horses.'

47. **Lob:** lop, hang dejectedly.

49. **gimmal'd:** jointed. See Robert Smith, 'Remarks on a Gimmal Ring,' *Archæologia*, XIV, 7–13.

50. **motionless.** They have not life enough to chew grass.

51. **executors:** possibly, executioners (as in i, 2, 203); but more probably in the modern sense—as executors settle the estates of dead men, so the crows will pick the bones of these horses (or horses and soldiers)—all they have to leave behind them. Cf. *Edward III*, iv, 5, 28 ff. (ed. Brooke, *Shakespeare Apocrypha*, p. 95).

53. **suit itself in words:** clothe itself in fitting terms.

54. **To demonstrate the life of such a battle:** to describe such an army *to the life*. Note the scornful playing on the word *life* in the next verse.

60. **guidon:** the pennant or little banner fixed to a staff—his official sign as commander. Cf. New Shakspere Society, *Transactions*, 1880–1886, p. 203; *ib.*, 1887–1892, p. 226.

61. **banner:** the streamer affixed to a trumpet.—**trumpet:** trumpeter.

63. **outwear:** waste in idleness.

Scene III.

2. **battle:** army drawn up.

6. **charge:** troop, division.

20. **enow.** See note on iv, 2, 28.

22. **God's will!** Comparing this interjection with *By Jove* in the next verse, Dr. Johnson remarks that 'the king prays like a Christian and swears like a heathen.' This is witty, but not sound; for *God's will!* and *God's peace!* (l. 31) are oaths, not prayers. Cf. Heywood, *Edward IV*, i, 1 (Shakespeare Society ed., p. 3): 'God's will, what chiding still?' Greene, *The Third Part of Conny-Catching* (ed. Grosart, X, 177): 'O Gods will'; Kyd, *The Spanish Tragedy*, p. 67: 'God's will that I should set this tree.'

26. **It yearns me not:** it does not trouble me.

36. **passport:** discharge and free conduct.

37. **convoy:** travelling expenses.

39. **fears his fellowship to die with us:** is afraid to grant me his company by dying with me.

42. **a-tiptoe:** on tiptoe (with enthusiasm).

44. **live:** outlive.

45. **the vigil:** the vigil of a feast is the eve of the feast day, the night before it, which was celebrated with merriment. Cf. Christmas Eve, which is the vigil of Christmas.

50. **with advantages:** with additions, with exaggeration.

57. **Crispin Crispian.** The Battle of Agincourt was fought on the day of St. Crispin and St. Crispian.

62. **vile:** of low birth.

63. **gentle his condition:** give him the rank of a gentleman.

68. **bestow yourself:** take up your position.

69. **bravely:** finely, handsomely—referring to the splendid appearance that they make.—**battles:** battalions.

70. **expedience:** speed.

76. **unwish'd five thousand men.** The English had about ten thousand men. The King's arithmetic has given the commentators some trouble. Apparently he regards himself and Westminster as each representing half of the English forces (as would indeed be the case if the two fought the battle alone), and thinks of Westminster as having wished his own half out of existence. But the passage is far from clear.

77. **likes:** pleases.

80. **compound:** settle, make arrangements.

82. **gulf:** whirlpool.

83. **englutted:** swallowed up.

84. **mind:** remind.

88. **fester:** rot.

91. **achieve:** win, get possession of.

107. **in relapse of mortality:** by a kind of indirect deadliness.

117. **They'll be,** etc.: they'll have fresher clothing (in some other way) or else they'll pull off the French coats for their own use—or, as we should say, they'll have fresher attire even if they have to pull off the French soldiers' coats to get it.

119. **turn them out of service.** With a pun, as if the French soldiers were servants in livery.

124. **as I will leave 'em them:** in the dilapidated condition in which they will be before I fall.

130. **vaward:** van.

Scene IV.

4. **Callino custore me!** Pistol does not understand French, but he catches the word *qualité* and echoes it in a distorted form, adding some strange words of his own. Malone conjectured that *calmie custure me* is a misprint for *Calen, o custure me*, which Boswell corrected further to *Callino, castore me.* These words

appear to be the refrain of an Irish song,[1] and perhaps we should restore them here. But it is perilous to emend Pistol's gibberish, and we have no warrant for supposing that he would not murder Irish as badly as he murders French in this play and Italian in *2 Henry IV.* He probably means to express contempt and to make an impression on the Frenchmen.

5. **Discuss:** declare!

7. **Signieur Dew.** Pistol takes the Frenchman's terrified exclamation (*Lord God!*) as a reply to his demand for his name. He recognizes *Seigneur* as meaning 'Lord,' and infers that his prisoner must be a gentleman.

8. **Perpend:** attend to, ponder.

9. **fox:** sword—so called because those made of a particularly good kind of steel had the figure of a fox as a trade-mark on the blade.

14. **Moy:** this Pistol takes as a sum of money or a coin. Some suppose he is thinking of a *moidore*, a Portuguese gold coin. '*Pardonez moy*' rhymes with 'anoye' and 'destroye' in Gascoigne's *Dulce Bellum Inexpertis* (*Poems*, ed. Hazlitt, I, 192).

15. **rim:** midriff, diaphragm.

19. **Brass.** The *s* in *bras* was pronounced in early seventeenth-century French, so that Pistol's error is not unnatural—for him!

20. **luxurious:** lascivious. Cf. Dekker, *Iests to Make You Merie*, in *Non-Dramatic Works*, ed. Grosart, II, 305: 'as lecherous as a mountaine goate.'

29. **I'll fer him.** Pistol simply repeats the soldier's name with a threatening air. Cf. Falstaff's words to the merchants in *1 Henry IV*, ii, 2, 96: 'You are grand*jurors*, are ye? We'll *jure* ye,

[1] Cf. Clement Robinson, *A Handful of Pleasant Delights* (ed. Arber, p. 33); Nashe, *Lenten Stuff* (ed. McKerrow, III, 177); Dekker, *Satiromastix* (Pearson ed., I, 260); New Shakspere Society, *Transactions*, 1880–1886, pp. 206–208; Southey, *The Doctor*, chap. xlviii (ed. R. B. Johnson, p. 340); *Celtic Review*, IX, 132.

faith!'—**firk:** beat.—**ferret:** worry—as a ferret does a rat. Cf. *Northward Ho*, v, 1, in Webster's *Works* (ed. Dyce, p. 276): 'The post-horse are ready; 'tis but a quarter of an hour's riding; we'll ferret them and firk them, in faith.'

39. cuppele gorge. This bit of broken French Pistol had learned before he set out for the war. Cf. ii, 1, 75, 76: 'Couple a gorge! That is the word.' Cf. Marlowe, *Jew of Malta*, iv, 5 (ed. Dyce, I, 322; ed. H. S. Bennett, p. 138): 'But, if I get him, *coupe de gorge* for that.'

40. brave: fine.

42. O, je vous supplie, etc. The Frenchman does not understand Pistol's lingo,—except 'Owy, cuppele gorge,'—but he finds his ferocious gestures intelligible enough.

68. As I suck blood: an oath—as truly as I am a bloodsucker! Cf. ii, 3, 57, 58:

> Let us to France, like horse-leeches, my boys,
> To suck, to suck, the very blood to suck!

71 ff. The Boy's soliloquy not only tells us of the sad fate of Bardolph and Nym, but gives us important information about the defencelessness of the English camp.

73. The empty vessel, etc. Cf. *King Lear*, i, 1, 155:

> Nor are those empty-hearted whose low sound
> Reverbs no hollowness.

75. roaring devil, etc. The devil in the moralities was a very boisterous character, but was constantly worried by the Vice, or clown, who used to offer to pare his long nails with his dagger, which was palpably made of wood. Cf. the Fool's song in *Twelfth Night*, iv, 2, 130 ff.:

> I am gone, sir,
>   And anon, sir,
> I'll be with you again,
>   In a trice,
>   Like to the old Vice,
> Your need to sustain;

> Who, with dagger of lath,
> In his rage and his wrath,
>   Cries 'aha!' to the devil.
> Like a mad lad,
> 'Pare thy nails, dad.'
> Adieu, goodman devil.

75, 76. **that . . . his:** whose.

Scene V.

---

3. **confounded:** ruined, lost.
8. **perdurable:** lasting—practically, eternal.
17. **friend:** befriend.
18. **on heaps:** in crowds.
19. **enow.** See note on iv, 2, 28.

Scene VI.

---

3. **commends him:** sends his respects.
8. **Larding:** enriching—with his blood.
9. **honour-owing:** honour-possessing, honourable.
11. **haggled:** hacked and gashed. Cf. Coryat, *Crudities*, 1776 ed., II, 53: 'I haue seene a Mountebanke hackle and gash his naked arme with a knife'; *ib.*, I, 35, II, 193, 249.
21. **raught:** reached.
23. **Commend my service:** give my love and duty.
31. **all my mother:** all the weakness that I inherited from my mother. Such apologies for weeping were a literary convention in Elizabethan English.
33. **I must perforce compound . . . issue too:** I am forced to make a compromise with my eyes, allowing them to be misty; otherwise they will insist on weeping outright.

35. **Alarum:** call to arms. This is the rally which the French nobles talk of in Scene v.

37. **kill his prisoners.** A savage, but necessary, order, since the prisoners might revolt, and the victory be changed to a defeat. Apparently, however, this order was not actually made effectual till the King learned that the French had massacred the boys and lackeys left in charge of the camp (see the next scene, ll. 9–10).

Scene VII.

5. **not a boy left alive.** Falstaff's witty page, then, perished in this massacre. Thus, of the old retainers of Falstaff, Pistol is the sole survivor.

11. **'tis.** *It* was often applied familiarly to *persons*, either in contempt or (as here) in affection.

12. **at Monmouth.** Fluellen remembers with pride that King Henry was born in Wales. Cf. 'For I am Welsh, you know, good countryman' (l. 110).

16. **the pig,** etc. Fluellen is touchy when his English is corrected, and displays his knowledge by uttering a string of synonyms.

18. **magnanimous:** great-souled, valiant.

19. **variations:** Fluellen's mistake for *various*.

34. **indifferent well:** pretty well.

34, 35. **there is figures in all things:** either (1) there is a symbolic likeness in all the events of their lives, or (2) literal agreement must not be expected, for we must allow for figurative language in making such historical comparisons. The latter seems better and is borne out by l. 46: 'I speak but in the figures and comparisons of it.'

36. **in his rages,** etc. Fluellen remembers Gower's criticism

of his English in l. 15 and once more (as in l. 16) displays his extensive knowledge of the English vocabulary. So also in l. 52.

59. **Until this instant.** The King's anger is caused by the massacre of the non-combatants and the pillage of the camp.— **trumpet:** trumpeter. 'I will the banner from a trumpet take' (iv, 2, 61).

62. **void:** abandon.

64. **skirr:** scurry.

69. **liege:** liege lord.

72. **I have fin'd these bones of mine for ransom:** I have limited my ransom to these bones of mine—I will give no more. See iv, 3, 120 ff. The repetition of the word *ransom* in the next line gives the passage a scornful effect.

79. **mercenary blood:** the blood of common soldiers, who fight for wages. The great nobles were supposed to render military service in return for their fiefs, not for money—though in fact, at this time, the practice had arisen (at least in England) of having contracts entered into between king and noble by which the latter received a definite sum in return for each soldier that he furnished. Still the personal service of the noble was not for money.

88. **peer:** appear, show themselves.

99. **pattle:** the Battle of Crécy.

104. **Monmouth caps:** a kind of cap much worn by the Welsh.

109. **a memorable honour:** an honourable memorial.

112. **Welsh plood:** Henry V's great-grandmother was a Welsh princess.

122. **just:** exact.

128. **should:** was to.—**withal:** with.

133. **take:** give. Cf. iv, 1, 231.

142. **quite from the answer of his degree:** quite exempt from

the necessity of accepting a challenge from a man of Williams's low rank.

143, 144. as good a gentleman as the devil is. Cf. *King Lear*, iii, 4, 148: 'The prince of darkness is a gentleman.' This was a proverbial saying. The Devil was obviously a person of rank, though fallen from his high estate.

148. Jacksauce: saucy fellow. In his excitement Fluellen's English becomes even more uncertain than usual. He uses *Jacksauce*, which is good English, in a very inappropriate way.

151. sirrah: merely *sir* with the *r* 'burred.' It is used as a familiar and sometimes a contemptuous term of address.

165. apprehend: arrest.

167 ff. Fluellen jets and struts like a turkey-cock.

188. touch'd with choler: when touched with anger.

189. injury: insult.

190. It is of course impossible for the King to allow Williams to strike him, for such an act would be high treason. Hence, in order to save Williams's honour, he devises this trick at Fluellen's expense. Of course Fluellen cannot be offended when he knows the truth.

Scene VIII.

---

1. Williams has just delivered the message which the King entrusted to him for Captain Gower in iv, 7, 158.

10. 'Sblood: a very round oath; literally, 'by the blood of God.'

10, 11. in the universal world, or in France, or in England. Fluellen's excitement betrays him into an anti-climax.

18. apprehend: arrest.

22. contagious: Fluellen probably means 'flagitious' or the like.

30. in change: in exchange.

35. saving your Majesty's manhood: an apologetic phrase on account of the abusive words which Fluellen intends to use. The meaning is, 'In what I say, I have no intention of insulting your honour.' Such phrases were common. The literal meaning is, 'your manhood being safe,' i.e., unassailed, not infringed upon.

38. **avouchment.** Fluellen uses this in place of the verb *avouch,* 'testify.'

44. **bitter terms:** bitter words.

53. **like yourself:** in your own attire, etc.

59. **I made no offence.** A regular Elizabethan idiom, like 'to make a fault.'

66. **By this day,** etc. As soon as Fluellen knows that it was all the King's joke, his resentment is pacified. It was, of course, an honour for him to act as the King's representative even if the King was taking liberties with his dignity. The soldier's spirited conduct was of a kind to approve itself to Fluellen's disposition.

69. **prawls,** etc. Fluellen's supply of synonyms still holds out.

72. **I will none of your money.** Williams is something of a grumbler and not so easily pacified as the more mercurial Fluellen.

75. **wherefore should you be so pashful?** Fluellen takes the soldier's reluctance to be the result of modesty. We must suppose that in the end Williams takes the shilling, though not with a very good grace.

85. **note:** list, memorandum.

93. **mercenaries:** common soldiers. See note on iv, 7, 79.

111. **But five-and-twenty.** This absurd number is actually handed down in the chronicles.

116. **Take it, God:** i.e., take the honour of it.

118. **in procession:** in religious procession.

122. **Is it not lawful,** etc. Fluellen, whose Welsh valour is mingled with an equally Welsh fondness for boasting, is a little distressed at the thought that the army is to take no credit for itself.

128. **'Non nobis' and 'Te Deum':** two well-known Psalms.

ACT V. Prologue.

What the Chorus is about to say is necessary information for those in the audience who have not read the history. For those who have, it may serve as a reminder of what is omitted on account of the impossibility of presenting all the details in the theatre.

10. **Pales in:** encloses as with a palisade.

12. **whiffler:** a whiffler was a person who went before the procession to clear the way. Here the sea seems in a similar manner to announce the coming of King Henry.

14. **set on:** advancing.

21. **trophy, signal, and ostent.** These three words mean much the same thing, but the first is the most definite. The second, meaning any kind of *evidence* or *sign* of victory, is somewhat less specific; and the third, *ostent*, meaning *show*, is the most abstract of all. We have here a fine example of the reversed climax.

22. **from:** the emphatic *from*, meaning 'away from.'

23. **In the quick forge,** etc.: i.e., in your imaginations.

25. **in best sort:** in their finest array, and with due ceremony.

26. **ántique.** Accented on the first syllable, according to Schmidt's rule.

29. **by a lower but loving likelihood:** to use a comparison which is somewhat less in dignity than the thing compared, but which nevertheless we use to show our love. The general referred to in l. 30 is Essex, who was now in Ireland attempting to subdue a rebellion. Since Essex was not so high a person as King Henry and the Irish wars were not so important as the French, the comparison is, of course, a lower one, but its employment testifies to the love which the writer has for Essex. As a matter of fact, Essex's return was quite different from that here hoped for.

30. **Empress.** A title much affected by Queen Elizabeth. Thus Spenser dedicates his *Faerie Queene* to her under this designation.

32. **broached:** spitted—as if rebellion were a monster which Essex was bringing home on the very sword which had pierced it. Cf. Marlowe, *1 Tamburlaine*, i, 2 (ed. Dyce, I, 22; ed. Ellis-Fermor, p. 80): 'bear empires on our spears.'

36, 37. **the lamentation of the French Invites the King of England's stay at home:** i.e., the French are in such despair that there is no occasion for King Henry to show himself in France at present.

38. **The Emperor:** i.e., the Holy Roman Emperor.

39. **To order peace:** to arrange terms of peace.

42. **There must we bring him.** This prepares the audience for the place of the next scenes, namely, France, and gives them to understand that in the meantime the King has returned to England and gone back to France again.

42, 43. **have play'd The interim:** i.e., have taken the place of the actors who would have represented what has gone on in the interval between Act IV and Act V.

43. **Rememb'ring you:** reminding you.

44. **brook abridgment:** put up with or be indulgent to our cutting down the full history.

Scene I.

1. **Nay, that's right.** As so often is the case, we hear only the end of the conversation. These two words refer to something which Fluellen has said; we have no means of knowing what.

3, 4. **There is occasions . . . in all things.** Cf. Fluellen's 'There is figures in all things' (iv, 7, 35).

4. **Ass:** Fluellen means *as*, which would ordinarily be spelled in Elizabethan English as we spell it. The spelling *ass* here indicates that he pronounced it *ass*, and so appeared to call Captain Gower by a very uncomplimentary name.

10. **yesterday:** i.e., on St. David's Day, when the leek was worn, as was customary on that day. St. David is the patron saint of the Welsh. Nobody knows how the custom originated. Cf. Rowlands, *The Common Cals, Cryes and Sounds of the Bellman* (*Works*, Hunterian Club ed., III, 264):

> I am no Welshman, but yet to show
> The loue I to the Countrey owe,
> I call this morning, and beseeke
> Each man prepare him for his Leeke;
> For as I heare some men say,
> The first of March is Saint *Dauids* day.

11. **It was in a place where I could,** etc. An example of such a place would be in the King's presence, in which it was improper for persons to engage in a private quarrel; but we need not suppose that this is what was meant here. There would be many other occasions on which it would be undignified and bad discipline for Fluellen to resent Pistol's insult.

20. **art thou bedlam?** art thou a lunatic? Pistol has misconstrued Fluellen's forbearance of the previous day and regards him as a coward. Furthermore, we should remember that Fluellen is probably not by any means as tall as Pistol.

20, 21. **Troyan.** *Trojan, Greek, Corinthian*, etc., were common terms in the mouths of such persons as Pistol.—**Fold up Parca's fatal web:** i.e., put an end to their life. The Parcæ were the Roman Fates. Pistol thinks of them here as weaving the web of a man's life. To *fold up* this web would then be 'to abbreviate the life.'

26. **affections:** likings.

27. **disgestions:** digestions—not a blunder of Fluellen's, for the form was common.

29. **Cadwallader:** Cadwallader the Great, the last of the Welsh kings, whom Pistol here takes pleasure in representing as a goatherd merely. Of course, this is an insult to all Welshmen.

36. **mountain-squire:** i.e., a poverty-stricken squire from the barren mountains of Wales.

37. **squire of low degree:** an allusion to a very popular metrical romance, composed in the fifteenth century and well-known in Shakespeare's time. Of course Fluellen means that he will humble Pistol. Cf. Nashe, *Pierce Penilesse* (in *Works*, ed. Mc-Kerrow, i, 169); Ford, *Love's Sacrifice*, iv, 1 (in *Works*, ed. Gifford and Dyce, ii, 81); Marston, *The Fawn*, ii, 1 (in *Works*, ed. Bullen, ii, 135).

40. **astonish'd:** almost equivalent to 'stunned.'

43. **four days.** *Four* was a common round number. Cf. *Hamlet*, ii, 2, 160, 161: 'He walks four hours together Here in the lobby.'

45. **ploody coxcomb:** bloody head. *Coxcomb* is a jocose and contemptuous name for 'head.'

55. **Much good do you:** a common blessing with one's meat.

57. **broken coxcomb.** Note that *to break one's head* was simply 'to draw blood upon one's head'—not, of course, 'to fracture the skull.'

60. **Good.** Pistol says this with all the awful significance of a threat, but Fluellen chooses to take it as if he had commended the leek which he is eating.

67. **I take thy groat in earnest of revenge.** *Earnest* is properly a small sum of money paid on the conclusion of a bargain to bind the transaction. Here, of course, Pistol means that he takes this money to remind him that he owes Fluellen revenge.

70. **God b' wi' you:** one of the numerous contracted forms of *God be with you* meaning 'good-bye.' The most contracted of all is that which we at present use, *good-bye* itself.

75. **upon an honourable respect:** on account of an honourable reason or consideration.

78. **gleeking:** poking fun.—**galling:** making satirical remarks. *To gall* is properly 'to excoriate' or 'to rub the skin off.'

80. **garb:** fashion.

84. **condition:** character. The meaning is, 'teach you how a good Englishman should behave.'

85. **play the huswife:** i.e., play the hussy, betray me. Fortune is constantly spoken of as an unfaithful mistress because she smiles upon all men but is constant to none.

86. **my Nell:** this would seem to be the Hostess. The Folios read 'Doll.' The correction is Capell's. Cf. Nicholson, in New Shakspere Society, *Transactions*, 1880–1886, pp. 209–211, 226.—**spital:** hospital.

89, 90. **from my weary limbs Honour is cudgell'd:** having been publicly cudgelled without instantly killing his assailant, Pistol's honour as a gentleman and a soldier was of course quite gone.

90. **bawd:** pander.

91. **something lean to cutpurse of quick hand:** i.e., show a certain inclination to the profession of Nimblefinger Cutpurse. This profession, as well as that of pandering, had been cultivated by Pistol before he went to the wars.

92. Note the repetition of the word *steal*, here with comic effect.

Scene II.

1. **Peace to this meeting, wherefore we are met!** Peace be to this assembly, and it is precisely for that purpose (namely, to make peace) that we have come together.

2. **France:** the king of France.

5. **royalty:** royal family.

16. **met them in their bent:** met them in their gaze.

17. **The fatal balls of murthering basilisks.** This line involves an elaborate double meaning. (1) The basilisk was a fabu-

lous monster of the serpent kind, which was supposed to kill by venomous emanations from its eyeballs, so that its glance meant death. (2) The name *basilisk* was also given to a certain kind of cannon, so called because originally it bore the figure of a basilisk.

19. **quality:** nature, essential quality.—**that.** The clause depends upon *hope* in the line before.

20. **griefs:** grievances.

23. **on equal love:** in consequence of the equal love that I bear to you both.

27. **Unto this bar.** There was a bar fixed between the French dignitaries and the English when the interview actually took place, and we must suppose that this was also represented on the stage.

29. **my office:** my good offices, my services.

31. **congreeted:** met together.

32. **before this royal view:** in the presence of these kings.

33. **rub:** an impediment—a technical term in bowling.

37. **put up her lovely visage:** i.e., raise it from the ground where she lies prostrate; or, perhaps, simply show her face, since the idea seems to be that she has been driven out of France.

42. **even-pleach'd:** even-plaited—i.e., with the ends twined in so as to present an even surface, as was often done with hedges. Cf. J. Hector St. John [de Crèvecœur], *Letters from an American Farmer*, London, 1783, p. 14: 'plashed hedges.'

44. **leas:** in the usual agricultural sense.

45. **darnel:** the tares mentioned in the Bible.

46. **while that:** equivalent to a simple 'while.' Almost every particle of the relative kind may be reinforced by means of a following *that*.

47. **deracinate:** uproot.—**savagery:** wild growths.

48. **erst:** formerly. The word is really a superlative from the same root from which comes the comparative form *ere*.

49. **burnet:** a kind of fodder.

51. **Conceives by idleness:** that is to say, is fertilized with useless weeds.—**teems:** brings forth. The object is *nothing*.

52. **kecksies:** a kex is a dry hemlock shoot or the like.

55. **Defective in their natures:** i.e., losing their true natures, which is to bring forth useful plants, and the like.

61. **defus'd:** disordered.

63. **favour:** good appearance, comeliness.

65. **the let:** the hindrance.

66. **inconveniences:** improper or unbecoming things.

68. **would:** here used as a transitive verb—if you would like to have.

73. **enschedul'd:** drawn up in the form of a schedule.

77. **cursorary:** cursory.

78. **Pleaseth your Grace:** a common polite form, equivalent to 'if your Grace pleases' or 'may it please your Grace.'

79. **presently:** at once.

81. **suddenly:** immediately,—containing the notion of rapidity without that of abruptness.

82. **Pass our accept,** etc. A peremptory answer—'settle upon what we can accept and give an answer which shall be final so far as we are concerned.' For this use of *pass* cf. 'to pass a law,' 'to pass a degree of rank.'

83. **we shall.** A most courteous form of assent in Elizabethan times—more so than 'we will,' because it does not imply, as the latter does, the exercise of any volition on the part of the person who consents.

88. **advantageable:** advantageous.

89. **in or out of our demands:** whether included in our demands or not.

90. **consign:** agree formally. *To consign* literally means 'to seal together with' and so 'to consent in a most solemn way.'

93. **Happily:** very likely, perhaps.

94. **When articles too nicely urg'd be stood on:** When things or demands, the mention of which is too punctilious or particular, are insisted on or made a point of. Note that *urged* means not 'pressed' (which is the sense of *stood on*) but simply 'mentioned'—a common meaning. *Nicely* means 'scrupulously,' 'punctiliously,' 'with too great attention to detail,' or 'an inclination to insist on trifles.'

98 ff. Cf. Chapman, *Alphonsus Emperour of Germany*, ii, 2 (Pearson ed., III, 216 ff.).

112. Katherine's readiness in understanding a compliment in English is a pretty touch.

124, 125. **The Princess is the better Englishwoman:** i.e., she has a true English modesty and common sense in the matter of trusting compliments.

128. **such a plain king.** As a matter of fact, the King was highly accomplished. He was anything but a farmer-like person. We have our choice, then, in the present case between two suppositions. Either Shakespeare (1) is describing a different kind of man from Prince Hal or (2) the King is representing himself as far plainer than he actually is.

130. **to mince it:** to mince matters, to speak delicately, like a courtier.

132, 133. **I wear out my suit:** I have used up my resources as a wooer.

133. **clap hands:** clasp hands.

138, 139. **you undid me:** you would ruin me.

141. **in measure:** a measure was a kind of stately court dance.

144. **under the correction of bragging be it spoken:** an apologetic phrase, 'let me speak it without incurring blame for bragging, for I do not mean to brag.'

146. **buffet:** box.—**bound my horse:** make my horse jump.

148. **jackanapes:** ape. The reference is, of course, to performing apes that ride horseback. As to the derivation of this

word, see C. P. G. Scott's article in the *Transactions of the American Philological Association*, XXIII (1892), pp. 189 ff.

149. **look greenly:** look foolish. The King's contemptuous phrase for the moonstruck, sentimental looks of lovers. Note the idiom: we should use the adjective, not the adverb, after *look*.

150. **cunning:** skill.

154, 155. **whose face is not worth sun-burning:** i.e., whose complexion is so rugged that the sun takes no pleasure in spoiling it.

156, 157. **let thine eye be thy cook:** the meaning of this phrase, which sounds proverbial, can only be guessed, but it must have been familiar to the Elizabethans. A cook takes plain material and dresses it until it forms an attractive dish. The King's face, he says, is plain. Let the Princess love him and that face will become attractive in her eyes. Thus her eyes may be said to invest his face with qualities which it does not possess by nature, as the cook prepares plain material by the exercise of his art. Other meanings are possible, but this seems to be the best.

157. **I speak to thee plain soldier:** i.e., the language that I use to thee is plain soldier's talk.

162. **uncoined:** sincere, uncounterfeited. A *coiner* was a false coiner or counterfeiter.

163. **do thee right:** be faithful to thee.

169. **will fall:** will fall away, will shrink.

175. **his:** its.

182. **you should love:** you would certainly love.

193. **Saint Denis.** The King swears appropriately enough by the national saint of France.

217. **a saving faith.** A common religious expression. Its use by the King shows how unsafe it is to infer that all such phrases were regarded by Shakespeare as Puritanical.

218. **with scambling:** by warfare (literally, 'scrambling'). Cf. *Respublica*, i, 3, 22, iii, 6, 42 (in Brandl, *Quellen des Welt-*

lichen Dramas in England, 290, 317); Gosson, *The Schoole of Abuse*, Shakespeare Society ed., p. 31; Marlowe, *The Jew of Malta*, i, 1 (ed. Dyce, I, 242; ed. Bennett, 43): 'we have scambled up More wealth by far than those that brag of faith.'

223. **the Turk**: the Grand Turk, the Sultan.

230. **bachelor**: young fellow, young knight.

239. **blood**: inclination, natural impulse.

240. **untempering**: unattractive. *To temper* often means 'to influence,' 'to work to one's will.' The King means that his face is not 'winning.'

241. **beshrew**: confound, curse.

244. **stubborn**: rude, rough.

253. **avouch**: declare.

257. **withal**: with.

263. **broken music**: a kind of music often mentioned in Elizabethan literature, but nowhere described. Perhaps it means the music of guitars and other similar instruments that are not played with a bow and give a more intermittent, or 'broken,' tone than the violin. Cf. Bacon's essay *Of Masques and Triumphs*: 'Dancing to song is a thing of great state and pleasure. I understand it that the song be in choir, placed aloft, and accompanied with some broken music, and the ditty fitted to the device'; Greene, *The Second Part of Tritameron*, ed. Grosart, III, 115: '*Iunos* feastes, as they begin with sweete Consortes, so they are intermingled with broken melodie.'

265. **break**: broach, utter.

293. **nice**: precise, punctilious.

295. **list**: barrier.

314. **condition**: character, ways.

336. **flies at Bartholomew-tide**. A proverb. Cf. Deloney, *The Gentle Craft* (ed. Lange, p. 8; ed. Mann, p. 75): 'as blind as a Flie in October, that will stand still while a man cuts of his head'; Middleton, *A Mad World, my Masters*, v, 1 (ed. Bullen, III, 338):

'like flies at Bartholomew-tide, that come up with drovers'; *The Changeling*, iii, 3 (*ib.*, VI, 49): 'a woman, they say, has an eye more than a man'; *Dick of Devonshire*, iv, 1 (ed. Bullen, *Old Plays*, II, 59): 'what a buzzing you make, as if you were a fly at Bartholomew-tyde at a Butchers stall'; Leigh Hunt, 'Coaches,' in *Essays*, ed. Arthur Symons, p. 117: 'The blind and staggering fly in autumn.'

344–346. **cannot see many a fair French city,** etc.: he means that, out of his love for Katherine, he is willing to give up many French cities which he might possess.

347. **perspectively:** as through a perspective glass—a kind of optical toy which distorts objects. It was in great favour with the Elizabethans and is often mentioned.

362. **According to their firm proposed natures:** exactly as they were defined in the terms proposed.

364. **Where:** whereas.

367. **addition:** title.

368. **Praeclarissimus:** most illustrious. This should be *praecarissimus*, 'very dear' (like the French *très-cher*). Shakespeare copied a misprint in Holinshed without taking the trouble to correct it.

373. **in:** out of, for. The common causal *in* used in adjurations. Cf. *in the bowels of the Lord*.

375. **daughter.** Some think the final *r* was trilled so as to make up the otherwise missing syllable at the end of the verse.

382. **that never war advance:** in order that war may never lift up. *Advance* in this sense is common. See ii, 2, 192, note.

387. **God, the best maker of all marriages.** According to the proverb 'Marriages are made in heaven.'

391. **ill office:** any unfriendly act.—**fell:** cruel.

393. **paction:** agreement.

Epilogue.

2. **bending:** bending over his desk; or, better, bending under the weight of the subject.

3. **room:** space.

4. **Mangling by starts,** etc.: depicting their glorious careers in disconnected fragments—as it were, by fits and starts.

7. **achieved:** won.

9. **infant bands:** swaddling clothes.

11. **had the managing:** i.e., had the managing *of.* The preposition at the end of a clause is often omitted in Elizabethan English.

13. **which oft our stage hath shown:** an allusion to the popularity of the three parts of *King Henry VI.*—**for their sake:** for the sake of those plays.

TEXTUAL NOTES

[Qq. indicates the exact agreement of two Quartos, Q₁ (1600) and Q₃ ('1608'). Q₂ (1602) is occasionally cited. Ff indicates the exact agreement of all four Folios, F₁ (1623), F₂ (1632), F₃ (1664), F₄ (1685). F₁ without mention of the others indicates agreement of the four except in some detail of spelling. The figures 1 and 2 after an editor's name indicate first and second edition. Conjectures are marked 'conj.'; omissions, 'om.']

Act i, Prologue, 9 spirits that have] Spirits, that hath (F₁ F₂ F₃); Spirit, that hath (F₄).
12 fields (F₁)] field (F₂); Field (F₃ F₄).
13 casques] Caskes (F₁ F₂); Casket (F₃ F₄).

Scene 1, 8 half] halfe (F₁); part (F₂ F₃ F₄).
19 pounds (F₁ F₂)] pound (F₃ F₄).
34 currance (F₁)] currant (F₂ F₃); current (F₄).
52 this (F₁ F₂)] his (F₃ F₄).

Scene 2, 27 wrong gives (F₂ F₃ F₄)] wrongs giues (F₁).
28 make (Rowe)] makes (Ff).
54 Then (Ff)] Thus (Qq).
72 fine (Qq)] find (Ff).
74 as heir] as heire (Qq); as th' Heire (F₁).
90 unto (F₁)] upon (F₂ F₃ F₄); vntil (Q₁); vntill (Q₃).
94 imbare (Warburton conj.; Theobald)] imbarre (F₁ F₂); imbar (F₃ F₄); imbace (Q₁ Q₂); embrace (Q₃).
98 is it (F₁ F₂ Q₁ Q₂)] it is (Q₃ F₃ F₄).
99 man (Ff)] sonne (Qq).
105 uncle's] Vnckles (F₁); Vncles (F₂); Vncle (Q₁ F₃ F₄); Vnckle (Q₃).
114 All (F₁ F₂ Qq)] And (F₃ F₄).
129 fields (F₁)] field (F₂ F₃ F₄).
131 blood] Bloods (F₁); Blouds (F₂); Bloud (F₃); Blood (F₄).
143 snatchers (Ff)] sneakers (Qq).
149 the (Qq F₁ F₂)] a (F₃ F₄).
163 her (Johnson conj.)] their (Ff); your (Qq).
166 West. (Capell)] Lord. (Qq); Bish. Ely. (Ff).
173 spoil] spoyle (Qq); tame (Ff); tear (Rowe₂).
175 curst (Qq)] crush'd (Ff).
182 Congreeing (Ff)] Congrueth (Qq).
183 True (Qq)] om. (Ff).
197 majesty, (Q₃)] maiestie, (Q₁); Maiesties (Ff).
198 masons (Q₁)] Masons (Q₃ F₁); Mason (F₂ F₃ F₄).
199 kneading (Ff)] lading (Qq).
208 Come (Ff)] Flye (Q₁); Fly (Q₃).
212 End (Qq)] And (Ff).

217 such powers (F₁)] that power (Qq).
222 well (F₁ F₂)] all (F₃ F₄).
233 waxen (Ff)] paper (Qq).
237 May't please (Ff)] Pleaseth (Qq).
243 are (Qq)] is (Ff).
271 as 'tis ever (F₁ F₂)] and tis (F₃ F₄).
276 that (Ff)] this (Qq).
297 you (F₁ F₂)] ye (F₃ F₄).

Act ii, Prologue, 20 see thy fault! France . . . out (Capell)] see, thy fault France . . . out, (Ff).
31 well] wee'l (F₁ F₂); we'll (F₃ F₄).
42 do we (F₁ F₂)] we do (F₃ F₄).

Scene 1, 9 is a (Qq F₁ F₂)] is but a (F₃ F₄).
11 an end (Ff)] the humor [humour (Q₃)] of it (Qq).
26 mare (Qq)] name (Ff).
39 drawn (Theobald)] hewne (F₁ F₂); hewn (F₃ F₄).
45 your (F₁ F₂)] thy (F₃ F₄).
53 nasty (F)] mesful (Q₁); mesfull (Q₃).
55 take (Ff)] talke (Qq).
65 doting (Ff)] groaning (Qq).
66] Qq add stage direction *They drawe* [*draw* (Q₃)].
75 Couple a] *Couple a* (Ff); Couple (Qq).
76 thee defy] thee defie (Qq); defie thee (Ff).
83, 84 enough. Go to (Pope)] enough to go to (Ff).
86 you, (Hanmer)] your (Ff).
87 face (Ff)] nose (Qq).
88 his (F₁ F₂)] the (Qq F₃ F₄).
93 home (F₁ F₂)] om. (F₃ F₄).
103 *They draw* (Qq)] *Draw* (Ff).
111 I shall . . . betting (Q₃)] I shall . . . beating (Q₁ Q₂); om. (Ff).
121 that's (F₂ F₃ F₄)] that (F₁); theres (Qq).
122 came (Qq F₂ F₃ F₄)] come (F₁).
123 Ah (Pope)] A (Ff).

Scene 2, 4 As if (F₁ F₂)] As if all (F₂ F₃).
5 loyalty (F₁ F₂ F₃)] Royalty (F₄).
9 dull'd (F₁ F₂)] lull'd (F₃ F₄).
25 was (Qq F₁ F₂)] was a (F₃ F₄).
29 *Grey.* (Q₃)] *Gray.* (Q₁ Q₂ F₄); *Kni.* (F₁ F₂ F₃).
29 True. Those] True: those (Ff); Euen those (Qq).
30 serve you (F₁ F₂)] observe you (F₃ F₄).
35 the weight (Ff)] their cause (Qq).

62 I (Ff)] Me (Qq).
75 hath (Qq F₄)] haue (F₁ F₂ F₃).
82 into (Ff)] vpon (Qq).
83 you (Ff)] them (Qq).
87 him (F₂ F₃ F₄)] om. (F₁).
103 stands (F₁)] stand (F₂ F₃ F₄).
104 and (Ff)] from (Qq).
107 a (F₂ F₃ F₄)] an (F₁).
110 on (F₁)] no (F₂ F₃ F₄).
114 All (Hanmer)] And (Ff).
123 might (F₁ F₂ F₃)] may (F₄).
139 mark the (Theobald)] make thee (Ff).
140 I (F₁ F₂ F₃)] and I (F₄).
148 Henry (Qq)] Thomas (Ff).
159 I (F₂ F₃ F₄)] om. (F₁).
160 and you (F₁ F₂)] om. (F₃ F₄).
176 have sought (Qq)] sought (F₁); three sought (F₂ F₃ F₄).
187 beginnings (F₁)] beginning (F₂ F₃ F₄).
188 on (F₁ F₂ F₃)] in (F₄).

Scene 3, 11 a finer (F₁ F₂)] finer (F₃F₄).
12 ev'n (F₁ F₂)] om. (F₃ F₄).
16 ends (Qq)] end (Ff).
17 'a babbled (Theobald)] a Table (Ff).
19 o' (Capell)] a (Ff).
27 as any (F₁ F₂ Qq)] as a (F₃ F₄).
27 so upward (F₃ F₄)] so vpward, (Qq); so vp-peer'd, (F₁); so up-war'd (F₂).
28 and all (F₁ F₂ Qq)] all (F₃ F₄).
35 *Host.* (Qq)] *Woman* (Ff).
44 and 'a said (F₁ F₂)] and [& (Q₂)] sed (Qq); and said (F₃ F₄).
44 hellfire] hell fire (Q₁ Q₂); hell (Q₃); Hell (Ff).
51 word (Q₁ Q₃)] world (Ff Q₂).
55 Caveto (Ff)] cophetua (Qq).

Scene 4, 4 and] and of (Ff).
43 cases (F₁)] causes (F₂ F₃ F₄).
75 brother (Q₁ Q₂)] brother of (Q₃); Brother of (Ff).
99 fiery (Walker conj.; Dyce)] fierce (Qq Ff).
106 Turns he] turnes he (Qq); Turning (Ff).
107 pining (Qq)] priuy (Ff).
112 too (Qq F₂ F₃ F₄)] to (F₁).
115 brother England (Q₁ Q₂)] brother of England (Q₃); Brother of England (Ff).
123 hot . . . of it (Ff)] loud . . . for it (Qq).

127 render (Qq F₁ F₂ F₃)] tender (F₄).
127 return (Ff)] reply (Qq).
131 the (Ff)] those (Qq).
132 Louvre] Louer (Qq F₁); Loover (F₂); Lover (F₃); *Louver* (F₄).
134 difference (Qq)] diff'rence (Ff).
137 masters (F₁)] musters (Qq).
138 That (Ff)] Which (Qq).
146 *Flourish*] after line 140 (Ff); om. (Qq).

Aᴄᴛ iii. Enter *Chorus*] *Actus Secundus. Flourish. Enter Chorus* (F₁);
Actus Secundus. Enter Chorus (F₂ F₃ F₄).
Prologue, 4 Hampton (Theobald)] Dover (Ff).
6 fanning (Rowe)] fayning (F₁ F₂); faining (F₃ F₄).
34 them (F₁ F₂)] him (F₃ F₄).

Scene 1, 7 summon (Rowe)] commune (Ff).
17 noble (Malone)] Noblish (F₁); Noblest (F₂ F₃ F₄).
24 men (F₄)] me (F₁ F₂ F₃).
32 Straining (Rowe)] Straying (Ff).

Scene 2, 20 Enter *Fluellen* F₁] *Enter* Flewellen *and beates them in* (Q₁);
Enter Flewellen, *and beats them in* (Q₃).
62 is not (F₁)] are not (F₂ F₃ F₄).
63 of the war] of the Warre (F₁ F₂); of War (F₃ F₄).
72 *Flu.* (Rowe)] *Welch.* (Ff) here and throughout the scene.
89 *Jamy.* (Rowe)] *Scot.* (Ff) here and throughout the scene.
93 *Mac.* (Rowe)] *Irish.* (Ff) here and throughout the scene.
93 Chrish, la] Chrish Law (F₁ F₂ F₃); Chrish, Law (F₄).
98, 122 la (Capell)] law (Ff).
114 Dukes. . . . no (F₁ F₂ F₃)] Duke. . . . not (F₄).
116 call (F₁ F₂)] calls (F₃ F₄).
127 that is (F₁ F₂)] om. (F₃ F₄).

Scene 3, 17 all (F₁ F₂)] of (F₃ F₄).
32 heady (F₃ F₄)] headly (F₁); headdy (F₂).
35 Defile (Rowe₂)] Desire (Ff).
43] Here Ff have: *Enter Governour.*
45 succours (Ff)] succour (Qq).
47 dread (Qq)] great (Ff).
54 all. For . . . uncle, (Pope)] all for . . . Vnckle. (F₁).

Scene 4. No attempt has been made to record any except the most important of the very numerous corrections and emendations in this scene.
1 parles bien] *bien parlas* (F₁); *parlois bien* (F₂ F₃ F₄).
8, 9 Et les doigts? *Alice.* Les doigts?] *Alice. E le doyts. Kat. Le doyts,* (F₁).

12, 13 *Kath.* La main ... escolier] *Alice. Le main ... escholier. Kath.* (F₁).
16 Nous] om. (Ff).
45 N'avez-vous pas déjà] *N'aue vos y desia* (F₁); *N'avez vous pas desia* (F₂ F₃ F₄).
47 mails] *Maylees* (F₁); *Nayles* (F₂ F₃ F₄).

Scene 5, 10 *Bour.* (Theobald)] *Bur.* (Qq); *Brit.* (Ff).
11 Mort de ma vie (F₂ F₃ F₄)] *Mort du ma vie* (F₁); *mor du* (Qq).
22 for (F₁ F₂ Qq)] for the (F₃ F₄).
22 land] Land (Ff); names (Qq).
23 roping (Ff)] frozen (Qq).
26 may (F₂ F₃ F₄)] om. (F₁).
32 *Bour.* (Theobald)] *Brit.* (Ff).
44, 45 Fauconberg, Foix (Capell)] *Faulconbridge, Loys* (Ff).
46 knights (Theobald conj.; Pope2)] Kings (Ff).
57 their (F₁ F₂)] the (F₃ F₄).
65 Not so, I (F₁ F₂)] Not so I (Qq); Not I, I (F₃ F₄).

Scene 6, 8 live (Ff)] life (Qq).
17 as (Ff)] om. (Qq).
21 Here is (Ff)] Do you not know him, here comes (Qq).
34 her (Qq)] his (Ff).
43 A damned (Qq)] a damned (F₁); damned (F₂ F₃ F₄).
82 suit] Sute (Ff); shout (Qq).
90 Hark] hearke (F₁ F₂); hear (F₃ F₄).
90 is (F₁ F₂ F₃)] his (F₄).
108 o'] a (Ff).
118 lenity (Q₃)] lenitie (Q₁ Q₂); Leuitie (F₁).
130 cue] Q. (Ff); kue (Qq).
157 thee, (F₄)] thee (Qq F₁ F₂); the (F₃).

Scene 7, 12 pasterns (F₂ F₃ F₄)] postures (F₁).
12 Ça, ha! (Theobald)] ch'ha (Ff).
14 avec (Nicholson conj.)] *ches* (Ff); *qui a* (Capell).
65 his (Ff)] her (Qq).
69 et la truie (Rowe)] *est la leuye* (Ff).
93 to hazard] to Hazard (F₁ F₂); Hazard (F₃ F₄).
149 such (F₁ F₂)] any such (F₃ F₄).
156 dare (F₁ F₂)] dare to (F₃ F₄).
168 o'] a (Ff).

AcT iv] *Actus Tertius* (Ff).
Prologue, 16 name] nam'd (Ff).
27 Presenteth] Presented (Ff).

35 his (F$_1$ F$_2$ F$_3$)] this (F$_4$).
45 Then (Theobald)] that (Ff).

Scene 1, 18 pains] paines (F$_1$);   pain [paine (F$_2$)] (F$_2$ F$_3$ F$_4$).
23 legerity (F$_1$ F$_2$)] celerity (F$_3$ F$_4$).
35 Qui va là (Rowe)] *Che vous la* (Ff); Ke ve la (Qq).
39 a gentleman] a Gentleman (Qq F$_1$ F$_2$ F$_3$); Gentleman (F$_4$).
43 a better (F$_1$ F$_2$ F$_3$)] better (Qq F$_4$).
62 *Manet King*] after line 63 (Ff); om. (Qq).
65 So!] 'So (Ff).
66 lower (Q$_3$)] lewer (Q$_1$ Q$_2$); fewer (Ff).
96 Thomas (Theobald conj.; Pope$_2$)] *John* (Ff).
103 is it not (Dyces$_3$)] it is not (Ff); is it (Rowe).
126 I (F$_1$)] om. (F$_2$ F$_3$ F$_4$).
149 in a (F$_1$)] in (F$_2$ F$_3$ F$_4$).
152 who (F$_1$)] whom (F$_2$ F$_3$ F$_4$).
187 do] doe (F$_1$ F$_2$ F$_3$); om. (F$_4$).
188 mote (Malone)] Moth (Ff Q$_3$); moath (Q$_1$ Q$_2$).
192 blessedly lost (Ff)] well spent (Qq).
198 ill (F$_1$ F$_2$ F$_3$)] ill is (F$_4$).
198 answer it (F$_1$ F$_2$)] answer for it (F$_3$ F$_4$).
209 You pay (Ff)] Mas youle pay (Q$_1$ Q$_2$); Masse you'l pay (Q$_3$).
211 and a (F$_1$F$_2$)]; and (F$_3$ F$_4$).
218 were (F$_1$ F$_2$ F$_3$)] om. (F$_4$).
232 take (F$_1$ F$_2$)] give (F$_3$ F$_4$).
246 *Exeunt* (Johnson)] at line 241 [*Exit* (F$_1$)] (Ff).
250 We (F$_1$ F$_2$)] He (F$_3$ F$_4$).
253 heart's-ease (F$_1$ F$_2$)] heart-ease (F$_3$ F$_4$).
262 What (Knight)] What? (Ff).
262 adoration?] Odoration? (F$_1$); Adoration? (F$_2$ F$_3$ F$_4$).
270 Think'st (Rowe)] Thinks (Ff).
275 That (F$_1$ F$_2$)] Thou (F$_3$ F$_4$).
283 ceremony] Ceremonie (F$_1$); Ceremonies (F$_2$ F$_3$ F$_4$).
308, 309 reck'ning, if . . . numbers Pluck (Tyrwhitt conj.; Steevens)]
reckning of . . . numbers: Pluck (F$_1$); reck'ning; lest . . . numbers Pluck
(Theobald).
324 Ay] I (F$_1$ F$_2$); om. (F$_3$ F$_4$).
326 friends (Qq)] friend (Ff).

Scene 2, 4 les eaux (Theobald)] *les ewes* (Ff).
6 Ciel! (Theobald)] *Cein*, (F$_1$ F$_2$); *Cien*, (F$_3$ F$_4$).
25 'gainst (F$_2$ F$_3$ F$_4$)] against (F$_1$).
25 exceptions (F$_1$ F$_2$)] exception (F$_3$ F$_4$).
47 dropping the hides (F$_1$)] drooping the hide (F$_2$ F$_3$ F$_4$).
49 gimmal'd] Iymold (Ff).

52 them, all (Rowe)] them all, (Ff).
60 guidon (Rann conj.)] Guard. On (Ff).

Scene 3, 6 b' wi'] buy' (Ff).
13, 14] These lines, which follow 11 and are Bedford's in Ff, were trans-
posed by Theobald at Thirlby's suggestion.
14 fram'd (F₁)] fam'd (F₂ F₃ F₄).
44 live . . . see (Pope)] see . . . liue (Ff).
48 (Qq)] om. (Ff).
49 shall (F₁)] shall not (Ff).
52 his mouth (Ff)] their mouthes (Q₁ Q₂); their mouths (Q₃).
59 remembered] remembred (Qq, Ff).
74 God's will] Gods will (F₁ F₂ Qq); God will (F₃ F₄).
75 could . . . royal battle] could . . . Royall battaile (F₁); might . . .
battle [battell (Q₃)] out (Qq).
87 all (Dyce₃)] off (Ff).
104 abounding (Ff)] abundant (Qq); a bounding (Theobald).
105 grazing] grasing (F₂ F₃ F₄); crasing (F₁ Qq).
113 will (Ff)] shall (Qq).
128 for (Theobald)] for a (Ff).

Scene 4, 4 Quality!] Qualtitie (F₁); Qualtity (F₂ F₃); Quality (F₄).
4 Callino (Malone)] calmie (F₁); calmy (F₂ F₃ F₄).
14 Or (Theobald conj.; Hanmer)] for (Ff).
38 à cette heure] *asture* (Ff).
43 suis (F₂ F₃ F₄)] *suis le* (F₁).
55 l'avez promis] *layt a promets* (F₁); *luy promettoz* (F₂); *luy promittez*
(F₃ F₄).
56 content de (F₂ F₃ F₄)] *content a* (F₁).
57 je (F₂ F₃ F₄)] *se* (F₁).
59 suis tombé] *intombe* (F₁); *ne tombe* (F₂ F₃ F₄).
60 distingué] *distinie* (F₁); *destiné* (F₂ F₃ F₄).
64 and he (F₁)] and (F₂ F₃ F₄).
69 me, cur] me cur (Qq); mee (F₁).
70 Suivez] *Saaue* (F₁); *Sauve* (F₂); *Suave* (F₃ F₄).

Scene 5, 3 Mort (F₂ F₃ F₄)] *Mor* (F₁ Qq).
3 de] Dieu (Ff); du (Qq).
11 Let's die in honour. Once (Knight)] Let us dye in once (F₁); Let
us flye in once (F₂ F₃ F₄); Lets dye with honour [honor (Q₃)] (Qq).
15 by a (Qq)] a base (F₁); by a base (F₂ F₃ F₄).

Scene 6, stage direction, with *Prisoners* (Ff)] Pistoll (Qq).
15 And . . . dear] And . . . deare (Q₁ Q₂); And . . . deere (Q₃); He . . . my (Ff).
21 raught (F₁ F₂)] caught (F₃ F₄).

27 noble] Noble (Ff); neuer (Qq).
31 And all (Ff)] But all (Qq).
34 mistful (Warburton conj.; Theobald)] mixtfull (F₁ F₂ F₃); mixtful
(F₄).
37 Then (Ff)] Bid (Qq).
38] Pistol ends scene in Qq: 'Couple gorge.'

Scene 7] *Actus Quartus* (Ff).
1 Kill (Ff)] Godes plud kil [kill (Q₃)] (Qq).
17 the great (Qq F₂ F₃ F₄)] the grear (F₁).
52 jests (F₁ F₂ F₃)] jest (F₄).
71 this, herald (Steevens)] this Herald (F₁); their Herald (F₂ F₃ F₄).
76 look (Collier₂)] booke (F₁).
81 the (Capell)] with (Ff); their (Malone).
113 pless it] plesse it, (F₁ F₂ F₃); pless, (F₄).
115 countryman (Q₁ F₂ F₃ F₄)] Countrey-man (Q₃); Countrymen (F₁).
121 God (Qq F₃ F₄)] Good (F₁ F₂).
132 'a live (Capell)] alive (Ff).
133 o' (F₄)] a (F₁); a' (F₂ F₃).
150 conscience, la] conscience law (F₁ F₂ F₃); conscience, law (F₄).
167 doo's (F₁ F₂)] do's (F₃); does (F₄).
182 o' (F₄)] a' (F₁ F₂ F₃).
185 his (F₁ F₂)] this (F₃ F₄).
190 no (F₁ F₂ F₃ Qq)] not (F₄).

Scene 8, 9 'Sblood] 'Sblud (F₁ F₂); 'Slbud (F₃); 'Sbud (F₄).
9 any's (F₄)] anyes (F₁ F₂ F₃).
69 to serve (F₁ F₂)] serve (F₃ F₄).
104 Fauconberg] *Fauconbridge* (F₁ F₂ F₃); *Fawconbridge* (Qq); *Faulconbridge* (F₄).
108–111 Edward . . . five-and-twenty] assigned to *Exe.* (Q₂ Q₃).
111–117 O God . . . only thine] assigned as if a new speech to *King* (Q₂
Q₃ F₂ F₃ F₄); F₁ begins a paragraph with 'O God.'
115, 116 loss . . . other? Take (Pope)] losse? . . . other, take (F₁).
117 only] onely (Qq); none but (F₁ F₂ F₃); none's, but (F₄).
118 we (F₂ F₃ F₄)] me (F₁).
129 enclos'd (Ff)] enterred (Q₁ Q₂); enter'd (Q₃).
130 And then (Ff)] Weele then (Q₁ Q₂); Weel (Q₃).
131 happy (Ff)] happier (Qq).

Aᴄᴛ v, Prologue, 7 There seen] there seene (F₁); And there being seene
[seen (F₃ F₄)] (F₂ F₃ F₄).
10 with wives (F₂ F₃ F₄)] Wiues (F₁).
29 lower but (Seymour conj.; Cambridge)] lower, but by (Ff).

Scene 1, 27 doo's (F₁ F₂ F₃)] does (F₄).

48] Q₃ adds the stage direction *He makes Ancient Pistoll bite of the Leeke.*

50 and yet (Grant White)] and eate (F₁ F₂); and eat (F₃); and, eat, (F₄).

70 God b' wi'] God bu'y (F₁ F₂); Gud bu'y (F₃ F₄).

75 begun (Capell)] began (Ff).

86 Nell (Johnson conj.)] Doll (Qq Ff).

87 malady (Pope)] a malady (Ff).

90 will I] Ile (F₁ F₂); I'le (F₃ F₄).

94 swear . . . got (F₃ F₄)] sweare . . . gat [got (Q₂)] (Qq); swore . . . got (F₁ F₂).

Scene 2, stage direction, *Burgundy* (Rowe)] *Bourgongne* [and in line 7 *Burgogne*] (F₁).

10 Fairly] fairely (F₁); faire (F₂); fair (F₃ F₄).

12 England (F₂ F₃ F₄)] Ireland (F₁).

35 plenty (Walker conj.; Dyce₂)] Plentyes (F₁ F₂); Plenties (F₃ F₄).

40 it (F₁ F₂)] it's (F₃ F₄).

42 even-pleach'd] euen pleachd (F₁ F₂); even, pleach'd (F₃ F₄).

45 fumitory (F₄)] Femetary (F₁ F₂ F₃).

50 all (Rowe)] withall (Ff).

54, 55 as . . . wildness, (Capell)] all . . . wildnesse. (F₁).

77 cursorary (Q₃)] curselarie (F₁); cursenary (Q₁ Q₂).

84 you (F₁)] om. (F₂ F₃ F₄).

93 Happily (F₁)] Happely (F₂ F₃); Haply (F₄).

98 and (F₁ F₃)] om. (F₃ F₄).

108 Pardonnez] *Pardonne* (Ff).

108 vat (Rowe)] wat (Ff).

120 the (F₁ F₂ F₃)] om. (F₄).

152 use (F₁ F₂)] us'd (F₃ F₄).

156 be thy (F₁ F₂ F₃)] be the (F₄).

159 Lord (Rowe)] L. (Ff).

180 you (F₁ F₂)] that you (F₃ F₄).

187 vat (Capell)] wat (Ff).

190 Quand j'ai (Pope)] Ie quand sur (Ff).

199, 200 que . . . est meilleur] *ques . . . & melius* [*melius* (F₃ F₄)] (Ff).

217 a saving (F₁ F₂)] saving (F₃ F₄).

239 notwithstanding (F₁ F₂)] yet notwithstanding (F₃ F₄).

252 your maiden (F₁ F₂)] those Maiden (F₃ F₄).

264 all Katherines (Capell conj.; Dyce₂)] all, Katherine (F₁).

266 sall] shall (Ff).

272 Laissez . . . laissez, laissez! Ma . . . abaissiez] *Laisse . . . laisse, laisse, may . . . abbaise* (Ff).

275, 276, d'une de vostre Seigneurie indigne . . . Excusez] *d'une nostre Seigneur indignie . . . excuse* (Ff).

284 it is not (F₁ F₂)] is not (F₃); is not to (F₄).
284 de] *le* (Ff); *les* (Theobald).
286 vat (Capell)] wat (F₁ F₂ F₃); what (F₄).
286 baiser] buisse (Ff).
289 It is (F₁ F₂)] Is it (F₃ F₄).
312 not (F₁ F₂)] om. (F₃ F₄).
332 consent (F₁)] consent to (F₂ F₃ F₄).
350 never (Rowe)] om. (Ff).
361 and in sequel] and in sequele (F₁); and then in sequele (F₂ F₃ F₄).
365 any (F F₂ Qq)] om. (F₃ F₄).
368 Praecarissimus (Warburton)] *Præclarissimus* (Ff).
393 paction (Theobald)] Pation (F₁ F₂); Passion (F₃ F₄).
398 we (F₁ F₂)] om. (F₃ F₄).

Epilogue, 12 made (F₁)] make (F₁ F₂ F₃).

GLOSSARIAL INDEX

foils, persons armed with stage swords, iv, Prologue, 50

footed, landed, ii, 4, 143

for, for want of, i, 2, 114; as for, ii, 4, 115; iii, 2, 34, 36, 38; iii, 3, 54; instead of, iii, 5, 60

force a play, ii, Prologue, 32

forehand, advantage, iv, 1, 297

forespent, previously spent, past, ii, 4, 36

Fortune, iii, 6, 26

four, an indefinite number, v, 1, 43

fox, sword, iv, 4, 9

fracted, broken, ii, 1, 130

France, the king of France, iii, 6, 166; v, 2, 2

friend, v., to befriend, iv, 5, 17

from, away from, i, 2, 272; v, Prologue, 22; exempt from, iv, 7, 142

full-fraught, fully-freighted, ii, 2, 139

gage, n., pledge, iv, 1, 223; iv, 7, 127

gall, n., resentment, ii, 2, 30

gall, v., to wear, iii, 1, 12; make satirical remarks, v, 1, 78

Gallia, France, v, 1, 94

galliard, a lively dance, i, 2, 252

galling, worrying, i, 2, 151

garb, fashion, v, 1, 80

gentle, v., to ennoble, iv, 3, 63

gentle(s), gentlemen and ladies, i, Prologue, 8; iv, Prologue, 45

gentleman of a company, an inferior officer, iv, 1, 39

gesture, bearing, demeanour, iv, Prologue, 25

giddy, fickle, untrustworthy, i, 2, 145

gilt, gold, ii, Prologue, 26

gimmal'd, jointed, iv, 2, 49

give o'er, to give up, iii, 2, 92

give place to, to give way to, retire before, iv, 1, 272

glean, to pick up by the way, i, 1, 53

gleaned land, i, 2, 151

gleeking, poking fun, v, 1, 78

gloze, to interpret, i, 2, 40

go about, to undertake, iv, 1, 212

go to, *interj.*, go away, ii, 1, 84

God be with you (b' wi' you), good-bye, iv, 1, 61; v, 1, 70

God before, with God's help, i, 2, 307; iii, 6, 165

God-a-mercy, gramercy, many thanks, iv, 1, 34

god-den, good e'en (evening), iii, 2, 89

God's will (oath), iv, 3, 23, 74

grace, n., virtue, i, 2, 242; honour, ii, Prologue, 28; mercy, iii, 3, 30; excellence, iii, 5, 34

grace, v., to honour, iii, 6, 71

grave, *adj.*, dignified, ii, 2, 128

greener, younger, ii, 4, 136

greenly (look), look foolish, v, 2, 149

griefs, grievances, v, 2, 20

groat, a fourpenny piece v, 1, 62, 63

gross, palpable, ii, 2, 104; stupid, iv, 1, 299

grossly, obviously, ii, 2, 107

guidon, a small flag, iv, 2, 60

gulf, whirlpool, ii, 4, 10; iv, 3, 82

gull, n., dupe, foolish fellow, iii, 6, 70

gull, v., to dupe, ii, 2, 121

gunstones, cannon balls, i, 2, 282

habit, attire (as a herald), iii, 6, 121

haggled, hacked and gashed, iv, 6, 11

half-achieved, half-won, iii, 3, 8

handkercher, handkerchief, iii, 2, 51

handle, to discuss, iii, 3, 39

happily, perhaps, v, 2, 93

happy, fortunate, i, 2, 300

hazard, a winning opening in a tennis court, i, 2, 263; a game at dice, iii, 7, 93

head, armed force, ii, 2, 18; (break), to break the skin of one's head, iii, 2, 42

heady, impetuous, i, 1, 34; iii, 3, 32

heaps (on), in crowds, iv, 5, 18

heart's-ease, contentment, iv, 1, 253

hilding, wretched, insignificant, iv, 2, 29

hilts, hilt, ii, Prologue, 9; ii, 1, 68

his, its, i, 1, 66; iv, 8, 14; v, 2, 175

Hold-fast, ii, 3, 54

hole in his coat, something discreditable in his record, iii, 6, 87

honour-owing, honour-possessing, honourable, iv, 6, 9

hooded (valour), iii, 7, 121

horse-leeches, ii, 3, 57

humorous, capricious, ii, 4, 28

humour, ii, 1, 63, 121, 127, 132, *etc.*

husbandry, thrift, economy, iv, 1, 8

huswife, hussy, v, 1, 85

Hyperion, the sun god, iv, 1, 292

Iceland dog, ii, 1, 44

idly, foolishly, i, 2, 59; (king'd), ii, 4, 26

if we may, ii, Prologue, 39

ill-favouredly, unbecomingly, iv, 2, 40

imaginary forces, forces of imagination, i, Prologue, 18

imagin'd, of the imagination, iii, Prologue, 1

imbare, to uncover, expose, i, 2, 94

imp of fame, scion of a famous stock, iv, 1, 45

impawn, to pledge as security, i, 2, 21

impeachment, hindrance, iii, 6, 151

imperial, i, 2, 35; ii, Prologue, 10

impounded, put into the pound, i, 2, 160

in, by, ii, 4, 102; into, iii, 6, 161; iv, 2, 10; out of, for, v, 3, 373

inconveniences, improper or unbecoming things, v, 2, 66
indifferent, impartial, i, 1, 72; (well), pretty well, iv, 7, 34
indifferently (well), tolerably, ii, 1, 58
indirectly, unjustly, ii, 4, 94
indued, endowed, ii, 2, 139
infant bands, swaddling clothes, v, Epilogue, 9
injury, insult, iv, 7, 189
instance, reason, ii, 2, 119
intelligence, spies, ii, Prologue, 12
intendment, intention, purpose, i, 2, 144
intertissued, interwoven, iv, 1, 279
invest, to clothe, iv, Prologue, 26
irreconcil'd, not atoned for, unremitted, iv, 1, 160
issue, *n.*, result, v, 2, 12
issue, *v.*, to shed tears, iv, 6, 34
it (*used of persons*), iv, 7, 11; its, v, 2, 40

jackanapes, an ape, v, 2, 148
Jacksauce, saucy fellow, iv, 7, 148
jades, nags, iii, 5, 19; iii, 7, 26; iv, 2, 46
jealous, suspicious, suspecting harm, iv, 1, 302
jealousy, suspicion, ii, 2, 126
just, correct, exact, ii, 1, 116; iii, 2, 7; iv, 7, 122; exactly so, iii, 7, 158
jutty, to overhang, iii, 1, 13

kecksies, dry stalks, v, 2, 52
keep, to maintain, i, 2, 273
keep close, to live retired, ii, 3, 64
kern, a light-armed Irish foot-soldier, iii, 7, 56
kill'd his heart, broken his heart, ii, 1, 92
kite, ii, 1, 80
knowledge (far out of his), away from any region with which he is acquainted, iii, 7, 144

lad of life, lively lad, iv, 1, 45
laquais, lackey, iv, 2, 2
lard, *v.*, to enrich, iv, 6, 8
large (at), in full, ii, 4, 121
late, lately appointed, ii, 2, 61
latter (day), last day, day of judgment, iv, 1, 143
lavolta, a high-capering dance, iii, 5, 33
Law Salique, i, 2, 11
lay, to bet, iv, 1, 242; (down), to plan, i, 2, 137
layer-up, preserver, v, 2, 248
lazar, leper, i, 1, 15; ii, 1, 80
lean, *v.*, to incline, tend, v, 1, 91
learn, to teach, iii, 6, 74
legerity, nimbleness, vigour, iv, 1, 23
legions, companies of devils, ii, 2, 124
let, hindrance, v, 2, 65

libertine, i, 1, 48
lie, to lodge, be encamped, iii, 7, 136
liege, liege lord, i, 2, 3; iv, 7, 69, 155; iv, 8, 26, 30
lieu (of), return for, i, 2, 255
lightly, easily, heedlessly, ii, 2, 89
like, in the guise of, i, Prologue, 5, 33; in the attire of, iv, 8, 53; likely, i, 1, 3
like, to please, iii, Prologue, 32; iv, 1, 16; iv, 3, 77
line, *n.*, pedigree, ii, 4, 88
line, *v.*, to strengthen, fortify, ii, 4, 7
linger (on), to hold out, ii, Prologue, 31
linstock, the staff that holds the gunner's match, iii, Prologue, 33
list, barrier, v, 2, 295
live, to outlive, iv, 3, 44
lob, hang dejectedly, iv, 2, 47
lofty, showy, high-mannered, iii, 5, 35
'longs, belongs, ii, 4, 80
low-rated, undervalued, iv, Prologue, 19
lustily, vigorously, iv, 1, 201
luxurious, lascivious, iv, 4, 20
luxury, lust, iii, 5, 6

magnanimous, great-souled, valiant, iii, 6, 6; iv, 7, 18
majesty, royal office, i, 2, 197
man, servant, iii, 2, 33
marches, borders, i, 2, 140
mary (marry), indeed, to be sure, iii, 2, 111, 128; iii, 7, 116
mean, persons of low degree, iv, Prologue, 45
measure, a stately dance, v, 2, 141
mechanic, *adj.*, i, 2, 200
meeter, more appropriate, i, 2, 254
memorable honour, honourable memorial, iv, 7, 109
men of mould, men of earth, mortal men, iii, 2, 22
mercenary, a common soldier who fights for wages, iv, 8, 93; (blood), iv, 7, 79
mervailous, extraordinary, ii, 1, 50
mettle, quality, iii, 1, 27
mickle, great, ii, 1, 70
mince, to speak delicately, like a courtier, v, 2, 130
mind (my), *n.*, opinion, what I think of him, iii, 6, 88
mind, *v.*, to conceive, see in the mind's eye, iv, Prologue, 53; remind, iv, 3, 13, 84
miscarry, come to harm, be lost, iv, 1, 155
miscreate, miscreated, spurious, i, 2, 16
mistress court, chief court in tennis, ii, 4, 133
modest, moderate, self-controlled, ii, 4, 34; (compliment), ii, 2, 134
modesty, moderation, iv, 1, 75

undo, to ruin, v, 2, 139
unprovided, unprepared for death, iv, 1, 184
unraised, uninspired, i, Prologue, 9
unspotted, not stained with guilt, iv, 1, 170
untempering, not ingratiating, v, 2, 240
up, to horse! iv, 2, 1
upon, as the result of, i, 1, 76; on the basis of, iii, 2, 84; on account of, iv, 1, 19; v, 1, 75
urg'd, proposed, i, 1, 1, 71; mentioned, v, 2, 94
use, personal advantage, ii, 2, 99

vacant, free from care, iv, 1, 286
vain, idle, i, 1, 54
vanities, follies, ii, 4, 36
vanity, frivolity, ii, 4, 130
vantage, advantage, iv, 1, 297
varlet, valet, a knight's attendant, iv, 2, 2
vasty, illimitable, i, Prologue, 12; ii, 4, 105
vaultages, caverns, ii, 4, 124
vaward, vanguard, iv, 3, 130
via, on! forward! iv, 2, 4
vië (*dissyllabic*), iii, 5, 11
view (this royal), these kings, v, 2, 32
vigil, the eve of (*i.e.*, preceding) a holy day or festival, iv, 3, 45
vile, of low birth, iv, 3, 62
visited, visited with God's vengeance, iv, 1, 187
voice, vote, ii, 2, 113
void, to abandon, iv, 7, 62
vulgar, common people, iv, 7, 80

wait on, to accompany, ii, 2, 110
wasteful, devastating, destructive, i, 2, 283; iii, 1, 14
waxen, engraved in wax and thus not permanent, i, 2, 233

we (*the royal*), i, 2, 4, *etc.*
what though, what of it, ii, 1, 9
whelk, knob, pustule, iii, 6, 109
where, whereas, v, 2, 364
whiffler, an officer who goes ahead to clear the way, v, Prologue, 12
while that, while, v, 2, 46
whiles, while, ii, 4, 57; iii, 3, 29, 30, 39; iii, 5, 24; iv, 3, 66
white-liver'd, cowardly, iii, 2, 34
Whitsun morris dance, ii, 4, 25
whoop, cry out, ii, 2, 108
will mistake, insist on mistaking, iii, 2, 146
wind up, to occupy and close, iv, 1, 296
wing (with the like), in similar flight, in the same way, iv, 1, 112
wink, to shut the eyes, ii, 1, 8; iii, 7, 153; v, 2, 327
wink'd at, disregarded, ii, 2, 55
with, by, iii, Prologue, 20
withal, with, i, 1, 81; iii, 5, 2, 12; iv, 7, 128; v, 2, 253; with that, i, 2, 216; at the same time, ii, 4, 34
womby, hollow, ii, 4, 124
word, watchword, motto, ii, 3, 51; order, iv, 6, 38
worshipp'd, honoured, i, 2, 233
wot, know, iv, 1, 299
would, would have, ii, Prologue, 18; would like to have, v, 2, 68
wrack, *n.*, wreck, wreckage, i, 2, 165
wrack, *v.*, to wreck, iv, 1, 100
wrangler, opponent, i, 2, 264
wringing (his own), that which pinches him, iv, 1, 253
wrong, wrongful acts, i, 2, 27

yearn, to trouble, iv, 3, 26; *see also* ern
yerk, to jerk, kick, iv, 7, 83
yet (*emphatic*), ii, 2, 57; iv, Prologue, 52
yield the crow a pudding, to die, ii, 1, 91